Yes, And

Lessons from *The Second City*

Yes, And

How Improvisation
Reverses "No, But"
Thinking and
Improves Creativity
and Collaboration

Kelly Leonard
&
Tom Yorton

HARPER
BUSINESS

An Imprint of HarperCollins*Publishers*

HarperCollins books may be purchased for educational, business, or sales promotional use. For information, please e-mail the Special Markets Department at SPsales@harpercollins.com.

FIRST EDITION

Designed by William Ruoto

Library of Congress Cataloging-in-Publication Data has been applied for.

ISBN: 978-0-06-224854-1

15 16 17 18 19   OV/RRD   10 9 8 7 6 5 4 3 2 1

This book is dedicated to the founders of The Second City and the generations of artists who honor the past by staying so fiercely in the moment.

ACKNOWLEDGMENTS

The authors wish to thank:

Viola Spolin, Paul Sills, Bernie Sahlins, Howard Alk, Sheldon Patinkin, Martin de Maat, Joyce Sloane, Cheryl Sloane, Nate DuFort, Jenna Deja, Monica Wilson, Robin Hammond, Alison Riley, Joe Ruffner, Dionna Griffin, Jeremy Smith, Beth Kligerman, Kerry Sheehan, Abby Mager, Matt Hovde, Klaus Schuller, Steve Johnston, Brynne Humphreys, Tim Mason, Steve Waltien, Christina Anthony, Ryan Bernier, Billy Bungeroth, Mick Napier, Diane Alexander, Tina Fey, Jeff Richmond, Steve Fisher, Peter Cunningham, Hal Lewis, Renée Fleming, Alexandra Day, Anthony Freud, Jeff Garlin, Michael Lewis, Elliott Masie, Betsy Myers, Dick Costolo, Dr. Mark Pfeffer, Eric Tsytsylin, Daniel Pink, Adrienne Kerwin, Alanda Coon, Eric Spitznagel, Hope Hudson, Stephanie Land, and Hollis Heimbouch.

Kelly and Tom would like to thank Andrew Alexander for telling us to write this book and for reminding us to manage and lead as improvisers, and Len Stuart for his never-ending support and mentorship

Kelly would like to thank his father and mother, Roy and Sheila Leonard, for saying "Yes, And" to his life in the theatre, his children Nick and Nora for their sheer wonder, and to Anne Libera for teaching him the true value of improvisation and directing him to be better at it.

Tom would like to thank his father and mother, Jim and Mary Yorton, for their stability and cheerful optimism, which made it possible for him to dream big; his wife, Maria, for encouraging his unlikely move back into the arts when others thought he was crazy; and his sons, Shane and Will, who motivate him to keep learning and stretching.

CONTENTS

INTRODUCTION

We have cool jobs. We get to work with generation after generation of some of the funniest and most creative individuals walking this planet. We work at a company that has established itself as an industry leader and our product is filled with invention, intellect, and laughter.

And sometimes we hate our jobs.

Everyone does.

But from our experience, we tend to hate them a lot less than other people. And we've been able to identify the core elements at play when we are happy in our work and when we are not.

We are at our happiest and most successful when we are working as improvisers. When we are fiercely following the elements of improvisation, we generate ideas both quickly and efficiently; we're more engaged with our coworkers; our interactions with clients become richer or more long-standing; we weather rough storms with more aplomb, and we don't work burdened by a fear of failure. When we are in full improviser mode, we become better leaders and better followers; likewise, we hear things that we didn't hear before because we are listening deeply and fully in the moment.

Our work and our lives are so much better when we act like improvisers. We are sure yours could be, too. That's why we wanted to share our stories; that's why we wrote this book.

We are not the creators of improvisational doctrine; we are not gurus; we don't lead Second City workshops or star in the productions. Yet for years we have been deeply involved in The Second City's efforts to help people become better at what they do by showing them how improv training can increase their capacity for innovation, their creativity, and their confidence. We are two people with vastly different professional backgrounds, and yet, independent of each other, we have witnessed enough at The Second City to arrive at identical conclusions: This stuff works, and this stuff works across myriad platforms.

Kelly grew up at The Second City, washing dishes and seating audience members when Mike Myers and Bonnie Hunt were virtual unknowns starring onstage in Chicago in the late 1980s. Although he thought he was working at The Second City as a way station prior to becoming a world-famous playwright (David Mamet held the same job at Second City some two decades before him), it turns out that he was something of an entrepreneur. When he moved to the box office in 1990, he pushed through a number of changes to better market the productions and improve customer service—despite an institutional reluctance to change anything. Promoted to associate producer of The Second City in 1992 at the ripe age of twenty-six, he sought out new talent for this world-famous theatre that had been experiencing a fair amount of criticism for artistic irrelevance. That fresh talent base included such young, unknown comic actor/writers as Stephen Colbert, Steve Carell, and Tina Fey. In 2001 he assumed the title of executive vice president of The Second City, where he devised new artistic and business opportunities with companies such as

Norwegian Cruise Line, developed partnerships with regional theatres across America to create original comedy plays, and forged alliances with Lyric Opera Chicago and Hubbard Street Dance to generate hybrid, commercial artistic events.

Tom is an advertising and marketing guy by trade who worked in ad agencies and client-side marketing positions before joining The Second City in early 2002. Always creatively overqualified for the jobs he let himself take, Tom jumped at the chance to run Second City Communications, now called Second City Works. Back then he won the beauty contest because the plan was to turn SCC into an ad agency. But we figured out how to be an agency of a different kind, one that did more than an ad agency by finding innovative applications for The Second City's core competencies of short-form comedy and improvisation. More on that throughout the book, but suffice it to say that Tom still gets to do what he's always done (find ways to win over audiences); he just uses a different tool kit to do it.

We decided to write this book together when we could no longer ignore the overwhelming evidence that our work was not only revolutionary, but that the revolution was already on its way. We wrote this introduction on February 23, 2014, the same day that the *New York Times* published an article by Thomas Friedman about the qualities that Google looks for when hiring, which include "the ability to process on the fly," a willingness "to relinquish power," ease with "creating space for others to contribute," and individuals who can "learn how to learn from failure."[1]

Those are the qualities of an improviser, and they can be learned. It is common knowledge that diet and exercise are keys to staying physically healthy, but practicing improvisation is like yoga for your professional development—a solid, strengthening workout that improves emotional intelligence, teaches you to pivot out of tight and uncomfortable spaces, and helps you become both a more compelling leader and a more collaborative follower. Even better, these qualities are fully transferable to your life outside the office. The benefits of improvisation can extend to your personal relationships, whether with your partner, your family, or your friends.

Anne Libera, former artistic director of The Second City Training Center, used to lead each orientation for beginning improv students with the same words: "This work will change your life." It has certainly changed ours for the better, and, based on the stories we hear from thousands of professional clients who credit their improv skills with helping them build effective teams, break down silos, foster creativity, and spark innovation, we're confident it can change yours, too.

So sit back, unwrap your candy, turn off your cell phone, and please refrain from taking photographs or making recordings of any kind. We take you now to a resort overlooking the Potomac River.

THE BUSINESS OF FUNNY

The Lansdowne Conference Center in Leesburg, Virginia, is a fine place to hold a business meeting, but located in the D.C. area wine country, with a hotel-style glass-and-brick facade and two championship golf courses, nobody would ever confuse it with a mecca for comedy. Yet every January for the past thirteen years, Lansdowne has rocked with laughter brought on by actors from The Second City who come to Virginia for an unlikely reason: to help about a hundred Major League Baseball rookies adapt to the unusual challenges of life in The Bigs.

These challenges are wide ranging and quite foreign to mere mortals who can't throw or hit a 95 mph fastball: how to deal effectively with veterans in the clubhouse and the rapacious media hordes, how to manage a newfound fortune when you grew up poor, how to find work-life balance when there is none, and how to navigate the perils of performance-enhancing drugs, aggressive autograph seekers, and the influence of organized crime in sports. Typical stuff for professional athletes, but not the typical fodder of comedy.

But Major League Baseball and the Major League Baseball Players Association know their audience (mostly guys around twenty years old, brimming with swag and testosterone) and because they know them well, they know that lectures and classroom finger wagging aren't effective ways to teach the vital life skills that will allow the rookies to have long and productive careers on the field. So they made the unlikely choice to bring in Second City talent who, over the course of four days, perform custom-written comedy vignettes based on real-world baseball situations, facilitate productive conversations around those vignettes (with Second City alum and clinical psychologist Dr. Kate Porterfield), teach improv-based communications skills, and in general, win over a tough audience of ballplayers who will be better equipped to protect their careers because of the time they've spent with a bunch of comedians and improv instructors. While our work at this conference is fun and funny, we're not brought in for mere entertainment. We're called on to bring serious topics to life through comedy, to get young athletes engaged, and to give them some important communications skills that will help them cope with circumstances few of us could ever truly understand. They do this because what The Second City knows, and what Major League Baseball has learned, is that the individual who is armed with an improvisational tool kit has an instantaneous advantage in dealing with all manner of difficult situations that naturally arise in the course of one's career. When, for instance, a long-lost third cousin once removed comes calling for a loan to start a deli/vinyl record shop, the young ballplayer will have learned improv skills to both disarm and deflect the advance—the same set of tools we'll give you to turn around difficult employees and disgruntled customers. Improvisation, at its most basic level, lets you respond more quickly in real time—and when practiced, also allows you to use comic relief to ease a potentially awkward confrontation.

Make 'em laugh. Make 'em think. A winning formula not only for baseball rookies, but for education reformers, cruise line directors, and the millions of other professionals whom Second City has reached over the past three decades by reformulating venerable theatre teaching methods into cutting-edge business training programs for the twenty-first century. We're not merely offering an improved communication tool, either. We've introduced a whole new skill set for invention and innovation that has been proven to unlock the creative forces of individuals and teams and make it easier for them to test those creative ideas and launch them in the marketplace.

The more The Second City works with folks from the business world, the more we have come to understand that despite all the planning, processes, controls, and governance, business is one big act of improvisation. For anyone who has spent time working in or running a business, you know that a great deal of your time and energy go to dealing with the unplanned and the unexpected, with the curve balls and gray zones that typify corporate life.

This book is for you, to help you build the tool kit you'll need to deal with that challenging reality.

SETTING THE SCENE

Maybe we're not brothers from another mother, but our comedy troupe and the businesses we work with have a lot of the same needs and priorities. We both work in teams that have to adapt to change and new information under high pressure and rapidly

changing circumstances. Just as businesses must create and innovate (or die), so must we, every night on the stage. We are both
ultimately accountable to the audiences we serve. Like our corporate clients, we must find and develop new talent to make sure our
business grows and stays vibrant over time. We face silos separating departments that would benefit greatly from a higher degree
of interaction and collaboration. When sales goals aren't being
reached or the competition steals away a client or that new product launch lands like a lead balloon, we are just as likely as others
to drop our best practices and work out of fear. The list goes on,
to the surprise of many, though probably to none more so than
the founders of The Second City. They could have had no idea
that their small cabaret theatre catering to University of Chicago
intellectuals and a burgeoning countercultural movement would
one day take its radical practices into the same institutions it ques-
tioned and challenged in the late '50s and early '60s.

When The Second City, housed in a converted Chinese laundry, first opened its doors on a snowy December night in 1959,
few attendees would have suspected that they were present at
the birth of an institution that would serve as the leading source
of cutting-edge comic artistry for the next half century. Today,
we take for granted that original comic voices have venues for
expression across all manner of stage and screen. But to understand how truly radical The Second City was when it launched,
we need to understand the cultural and artistic landscape at the
time.

"My wife will buy anything marked down. Last year she
bought an escalator." Such was the flavor of popular comedy in
the late '50s. Henny Youngman, Jack Benny, George Burns, Lu-
cille Ball, Jackie Gleason—all very funny, even legendary, comedians, but none of them satirists. Their comedy, rooted in the
inherent funniness of relationships and family dynamics, was

never vulgar or political. By the late '50s, however, a new breed of comedians appeared on the scene—Lenny Bruce, Mort Sahl, and Dick Gregory, for example—who would become part of the countercultural movement of the 1960s. Playing clubs such as Mister Kelly's and The Gaslight Club in Chicago, The Hungry i and North Beach Nightclub in San Francisco, and The Bitter End and The Duplex in New York, these new voices of stand-up represented an entirely different kind of comedy. They talked openly about sex, race, and politics, and, in the case of Lenny Bruce, they got thrown in jail for the profane language they used onstage. Prior to this movement, popular comedy was seen mostly as entertainment or diversion—rarely as part of an artistic movement that promoted social and political change.

The founders of The Second City—Paul Sills, Bernie Sahlins, and Howard Alk, all University of Chicago graduates—approached their work on two important fronts. They created a new form for the comic arts: ensemble based and rooted in the improvisational games that Sills's mother, Viola Spolin, taught as a social worker for a WPA-sponsored program on Chicago's South Side, designed to help immigrant children assimilate into their new culture. At the same time, in terms of content, these artists used comedy as a way to challenge the status quo. They combined both to react directly to the Eisenhower era—which they saw as conformist, intellectually bereft, and morally bankrupt—often shocking audiences in the process. The comedy they were creating was rooted in truth, rather than broad parody or exaggeration; the behavior they portrayed onstage was real and recognizable.

For example, in the classic 1961 Second City scene, "Family Reunion," a son, Warren, who moved to Chicago, welcomes his parents to the apartment he has shared with his roommate, Ted, for twelve years. The apartment gives every indication that it is shared by a couple, but the parents just won't see it. Warren finally summons the courage to tell his parents the truth:

> **WARREN** There's something I want to tell you about myself. I hope you want to hear something about myself. I'm—I—Ted is a homosexual.
> **FATHER** Well, Warren, I'm glad to see that living in the city has taught you tolerance.

That scene was startling to audiences when it was staged in 1961, but it ushered in a kind of comedy that blended the personal and the political.

Form and content: At The Second City, they are linked, and the more powerful for that. In an improvised art form, the actors are also the writers; they create their content in concert with their fellow ensemble members and in an ongoing dialogue with their audience. In addition, they abide by an old saying in the field: "It's funny because it's true." This compels them to draw from their personal experiences and to share true feelings and insights, both what brings them joy and what keeps them up at night. For the first generation of Second City artists, improvisation became the vehicle for a new kind of comic self-expression unlike anything that had come before. The work was funny, honest, and, because it dealt often in the most serious of subject matter, revolutionary.

Over the next half century, The Second City continued to challenge convention while further developing teaching methods, tools, and techniques that would turn it into an eagerly sought-out, creative beacon that attracted many of the country's brightest future comic stars—from Bill Murray to Gilda Radner, John Candy to John Belushi, Steve Carell to Tina Fey—each honing his or her craft in classes and onstage in The Second

City's touring and resident ensembles. Along the way, however, a new breed of performer also began seeking out The Second City: managers, marketers, teachers, lawyers, advertising executives, and business school graduates. Even politicians and daytime television hosts found their way into the entry-level improv classes that filled up The Second City's classrooms on weeknights and weekend days. (Oprah Winfrey's Second City classmates probably didn't realize that she might be using her improv training for some greater purpose than to get on *Saturday Night Live* when she took classes in the mid-1980s.)

While many of these individuals took classes at The Second City as a fun diversion or a way to meet people, it quickly became apparent to them that The Second City had much more to offer the world than mere entertainment. Whether they were looking to innovate more quickly, seeking a performance edge, hoping to improve teamwork and collaboration in their business units, become better presenters, or learn how to adapt to the change that is inevitable in every business, they found that The Second City's improv-based training approach was a potent way to build the essential skills that separate the stars from the also-rans in the corporate world. We were stunned, amazed, and more than a little surprised that our humble theatre, which had made its reputation as a place that took on authority figures and challenged "the man," could also be a place where "the man" learned how to develop professionally. Elliott Masie, CEO and founder of the MASIE Center, a think tank devoted to corporate learning, thinks the explanation could be due to a gap in the traditional B-school curriculum. As he explains, "It's about filling the room with truth and trust rather than just with loudness and noise. Laughter can be a big part of that. The one piece they don't teach in business school is the role of laughter and humor, [yet] I can't think of a single important contract, acquisition, sale, event—

for that matter, any hiring or firing that I've done—when there hasn't been some humor in it, or some laughter."[2]

So after many years of working in an ad hoc but increasingly successful way with corporate clients, we decided to create within the company a division dedicated to working with the business world; in 1989 The Second City Comedy Marketing Group, later renamed Second City Works, was born. Although it was originally developed as the company's corporate entertainment arm, over the past decade Second City Works has become a training ground for individual professionals and teams increasingly confounded by the amount of information they are expected to process, the speed at which industries, technology, and markets change, the volatility of the workplace, and the new standards for transparency and customer engagement. More and more people are recognizing what we at The Second City have known for a long time: Professional success often rests on the same pillars that form the foundation of great comedy improv: Creativity, Communication, and Collaboration.

SEVEN ELEMENTS OF IMPROV

While there's nothing wrong with the quantitative, strategic, and analytical skills traditionally taught at B-schools, those alone do not guarantee success in business, where things tend to be messier and more fluid, and where success often rests on the ability to form winning coalitions that will back a good idea. Here, the soft skills—such as a willingness to listen, forge trusting relationships, take and support responsible risks, adapt to change, and stay positive in the face of adversity—are seen as those essential to allowing people and businesses to respond with agility and nimbleness to the fast-moving information, op-portunities, and challenges of today's workplace. These skills are no longer merely nice to have—they are paramount. And they can be learned, using the same seven elements of improvisation that have inspired some of the most brilliant creative performers of our time.

1. Yes, And

These two words form the bedrock of all improvisation. Creative breakthroughs occur in environments where ideas are not just fully explored, but heightened and stretched to levels that might seem absurd at first. That is where the best comedy comes from, and that's where invention is realized. It's a mantra to apply at every level of your work. Work cultures that embrace Yes, And are more inventive, quicker to solve problems, and more likely to have engaged employees than organizations where ideas are judged, criticized, and rejected too quickly. With Yes, And, you don't have to act on every idea, but you do have to give every idea a chance to be acted on. This simple idea has amazing power and potency to improve interpersonal communication, negoti-ation, and conflict resolution. In application, these two words are ground zero to creativity and innovation. We will show you ways to incorporate Yes, And into almost every aspect of your business, and we will offer a none-too-subtle suggestion that this approach can work wonders in your personal life as well.

2. Ensemble

We celebrate the stars who break out at The Second City, but they didn't become stars by working as solo acts; they did it by learning to work in groups. The ensemble is the preeminent focus of everything in our business, and it pops up everywhere—in sales teams, executive boards, retail staff—and it is a vital ingredient in almost any organization's growth and competitiveness. Unfortunately, shockingly little attention is paid to building, maintaining, and developing ensembles. The consequences of that oversight are all around us, from the conference room full of smart people more interested in showing off their brain power than actually solving a problem, to the leader who takes credit for success and dodges accountability for failure, to the individual who whitewashes all his or her problems.

There is a way to reconcile the needs of individuals with those of the broader team. In fact, you can strengthen both at the same time. It's not a zero-sum game. Whether onstage or in business, stars can emerge out of high-functioning ensembles when all members address its main enemies: the need to be right, the need to steal focus, and the need to appear in control even when the evidence is otherwise. We will show you how to encourage good ensembles that yield great performance by creating an environment where the group's goals trump the individual's, where there's enough credit for all, and where candor is rewarded, not punished. In addition, we will show you how performing well within an ensemble can lay the path to your own stardom.

3. Co-Creation

Half a century of doing this work has shown us that dialogues push stories further than monologues. Our ensembles create art not only in front of the audience, but also in tacit conversation with the audience—seeking suggestions, monitoring feedback, and transforming material in turn. The sum of co-creation is greater than its parts. And in our increasingly connected world, co-creation is fast become a fact of life. Unfortunately, it is not usually taught or applied in the very corners where it is needed most. Yet using the improv methodologies in this book, you can learn to co-create new content and products, new marketing campaigns, new processes, and even new relationships between divisions and departments.

4. Authenticity

When people laugh, they're often laughing at the shared truth in the room. Unfortunately, truth is too often ignored or soft-pedaled in business out of fear of political incorrectness or for the sake of expediency. An adage that has helped guide The Second City through the years is "Dare to offend." We teach our performers to be unafraid to speak to power, to challenge conventions, and to question the rules.

The business or organization that takes itself too seriously and doesn't know how to question its own beliefs is at a strong competitive disadvantage. Rather than pretend that problems and failures don't exist, strong leaders and organizations acknowledge what's not working. They encourage team members to demonstrate their respect for the organization by questioning the status quo, challenging assumptions and traditions that may not be working, and calling out the truth, even when the truth is hard to hear. By allowing team members to air grievances or highlight problems, managers are better able to learn and grow. Unlike organizations married to hierarchy and the status quo, they are also better able to protect themselves from competitors who have embraced irreverence and therefore increased their innovation.

The line between respect and reverence isn't always easy to see, and we are continually faced with finding the balance between the two. But individuals and companies who can inject a healthy amount of irreverence into their corporate culture will not only improve their organization's morale, they will also be setting a foundation for being more competitive. Comedy and irreverence are lubricants that encourage people to reconsider long-standing beliefs that may be holding them back.

5. Failure

Failure is more than an abstract tenet for us. It is something we commit to every time we walk onstage. Counterintuitively, failure is something we actually practice when we improvise, as we look for our chance to "fall into the crack in the game," a term coined by Second City alum and teacher Rick Thomas. It's that moment onstage when a mistake happens—the whole audience knows it, and most of the actors onstage know it. But by acknowledging the mistake and incorporating it into the narrative, something new and unexpected happens that makes the audience go wild.

Too often we are told that failure is not an option. But the opposite is true. It's vital to give failure a role in your process. The biggest threat to creativity is fear, especially the fear of failure. By deflating the negative power of failure, you erode fear and allow creativity to flourish. This book will teach you how to get beyond the usual lip service paid to matters of risk and create safe opportunities for incremental failures that will lead to great successes.

Moreover, how organizations talk about failure can be key to how well they do. Companies that reflexively whitewash or punish failures create environments where nobody wants to take a chance or speak openly. Failure should be a given. There are ways to fully bake it into any creative process so that individuals aren't paralyzed when it happens, but rather see it as a necessary and even interesting means to an end.

6. Follow the Follower

In the late 1950s and early 1960s, two luminaries in vastly different fields hit upon a similar idea. Management consultant Peter Drucker introduced the concept of the knowledge worker and suggested that the success of any organization in the future would depend heavily on a flat organizational structure and management that allowed individuals to explore and live up to their potential. Around the same time, Viola Spolin, a pioneer of American theatre who literally wrote the book on improvisation, proposed "Follow the Follower" as a more active and dynamic way to provide leadership while working within an ensemble. It is a principle that gives the group the flexibility to allow any member to assume leadership for as long as his or her expertise is needed, and then to shuffle the hierarchy again once the group's needs change. At The Second City, we know that both of these creative thinkers were right. The success we've seen onstage has never come from a hierarchical construct, but rather from allowing each member of the ensemble—our knowledge workers, who each bring a particular expertise to the group—to take the reins when necessary.

Leadership is more about understanding status than about maintaining status. In other words, it's about recognizing the great power that comes in giving up the role of top dog on occasion. This is especially true in a global, web-enabled economy, where experts come together and disband frequently. In this world, leadership and expertise are more dynamic and a Follow the Follower approach leads to more success; leaders are able to empower teams of individuals who can bring their own ideas and their own creativity to the task of building the business. On any given day, in any given project, an employee might assume a leadership role, provide support, or liaise outside the group. Your organization will be stronger when it no longer relies on a single leader to initiate every new idea, but rather enables the creative minds of all its members to participate in the company's ongoing growth.

The ability to knowingly shift status inside the group dynamic is an art—and it doesn't come easily. In this book, we'll show you how to practice Follow the Follower so that you can strengthen your organization as well as your role within it.

7. Listening

Deep listening is essential to improvisation. It is also critical in many parts of business, from selling situations to employee evaluations to brainstorming sessions and more. In other words, the care and feeding of our listening muscle is an absolute priority for anyone who wishes to create, communicate, lead, or manage effectively.

Many of us believe that we are good listeners, but there is a huge difference between listening to understand and listening while waiting for the chance to respond. One enriches and broadens our perspective; the other feeds our need to be right and in control of the conversation. Unfortunately, most of the world operates in the listening-to-respond mode. The results are unimpressive. There's a better way.

Listening keeps you in the moment, not looking backward or jumping three steps ahead. Using a variety of Second City techniques, you can fill your workplace with individuals who know how to make their listening more active and, therefore, far more creative.

HERE'S YOUR TAKEAWAY

These seven elements are at the heart of The Second City's success and have contributed in no small part to the success stories of our famous alumni. They have also made their way into companies and organizations as diverse as Nissan, Motorola, Google, Nike, and McDonald's. Now, with this book, they can be yours.

At The Second City, we do not teach you how to be funny. You don't learn jokes or one-liners. Rather, you learn to tap into the part of your brain that so often censors the truth for fear of being judged. When people no longer feel limited to saying what is right or polite—when they are given freedom to express themselves in public, without inhibition or fear—that's when the funny happens.

To put it most simply, comedy provides us a safe place to speak and hear the truth. Unfortunately, at our most important moments, especially in the boardroom where the fate of a company may hang in the balance, freedom to speak the truth and, just as vitally, *hear* the truth, rarely exists.

This book can change all that. It will teach you not only the tools of an improviser, it will also explain how you can use comedy to communicate honestly and openly, especially during the most difficult conversations. Just like improvisation, comedy is a craft that requires technique and methodology. By exploring the seven elements of improvisation, *Yes, And* will enable you to find fresh, unconventional, and inspiring ways to:

- Generate ideas more quickly.
- Communicate more effectively.
- Create ensembles that rise to every occasion.
- Create open dialogue with employees and with customers.
- Break down organizational silos that threaten collaborative success.
- Make something out of nothing.

And those aren't just empty promises. We'll walk you through some specific ways we've been putting these ideas to work in all kinds of companies. We'll share the story of Farmers Insurance, which has embraced improv communications principles for years to help its claim reps become more effective and empathetic communicators in times of stress. We'll talk about the great results Clorox got when it let audience members co-create a marketing program with them via a live Twitter takeover on the web. And we'll discuss how we've helped a wide variety of Fortune 1,000 companies use comedy to engage their people on the traditionally dull and dreadful topic of . . . wait for it . . . compliance training.

What started as a small cabaret theatre in the heart of Chicago's Old Town is now a full-blown innovation laboratory where individuals and organizations routinely churn out the unexpected and unusual connections that lead to creative breakthroughs and paradigm shifts. Packed with stories that reveal a rare peek into the DNA of the world's most famous comedy institution, *Yes, And* offers specific improvisational methods and techniques that have been proven to help anyone become more innovative, more creative, and more successful in business, and in life.

YES, AND: HOW TO MAKE SOMETHING OUT OF NOTHING

A few years ago, Second City Works had the opportunity to work with a young HR manager at a global technology company (we'll call her Katie) who was chosen to participate in the company's "High Potentials" executive development program. The program was two years long and required participants to rotate into new jobs within the company every six months, which, in turn, required participants to be comfortable networking and assimilating regularly into new groups of people. Katie was bright, skilled, and highly motivated, but also somewhat introverted and terrified by the prospect of having to join entirely new teams and make productive connections with new coworkers every six months. She was typically reserved in new situations and didn't consider herself a networker who could plug into new teams easily. Katie worried that her lack of networking skills would limit her success and ultimately hurt her career.

Until we were brought in to work with Katie and her colleagues, she didn't know much about The Second City, and she certainly wouldn't have described such an exercise in peer networking as an act of improvisation. But to us, looking at Katie's situation through the lens of our stage work, the challenges that she and her peers faced were Improv 101. In improv parlance, Katie was having trouble initiating a scene because she was afraid she'd have to carry the scene all by herself. She was also intimidated by the idea of having to be interesting and compelling in each new situation right off the bat. She found herself in an improvisational situation, tasked with the responsibility of repeatedly creating something out of nothing, without the perspective or the tools to cope with it effectively.

So what did we have Katie do? Something very simple. We had her play a game called Exposure. The workshop instructor had Katie and half of the class go up and stand in a line on the stage while the rest of the class stayed in the audience, about ten feet away. The instructor then told each group, "You look at us, and we'll look at you." That's when the squirming started—and it wasn't just Katie. The whole group onstage started to shift their feet. Some got red in the face while others fussed with their hands and clothing. As soon as everyone in the group was displaying some degree of discomfort, the instructor spoke. "Now I want you to count every brick in the wall that you can see." Within seconds, the fidgeting stopped. Now everyone had a task to do. Each individual was concentrating. Within minutes, Katie and the rest of her group were smiling, completely at ease, as they attempted to count the number of bricks in the wall of the theatre.

What improvisation does, in its most simple form, is to take the focus off ourselves and allow us to dial down our personal judgment. When we're concentrating hard and fully present in the moment, there's no room for self-consciousness or shaky nerves. All your energy goes into the task at hand. This exercise allowed Katie to learn that even when she felt as if all eyes were upon her, if she just focused on getting her job done—in her case, networking and adapting to new divisions in her organization—she would be able to control her anxiety. In time, as she started to enjoy the fruits of her efforts, she would also realize that she was the only person judging her "performance," and she'd get more comfortable with the process.

As Katie loosened up, we added games that focused on improving her listening, sharing, and exchanging—all beginning-level improvisational exercises that work like calisthenics for your social skills. As Dr. Mark Pfeffer, a psychotherapist and director of the Panic/Anxiety Recovery Center in Chicago, explains, "Every time you learn to be unafraid, your brain changes. [Improv is] the quickest way to get to the neural pathway change, because it puts [people] in a situation where they're facing their fears."[3] Ultimately, Katie learned that she did in fact have all the communication and networking skills she thought she didn't possess. She just needed a place to practice them.

Mostly, though, she learned how to Yes, And.

WHAT IS YES, AND?

We've met a lot of Katies in our work, and over the years we've come to believe that no matter what title is on your business card, professional success requires the ability to create something out of nothing, which is in many ways at the heart of what it means to improvise. Katie was trying to create new, effective professional relationships out of nothing, but the list of things business professionals have to create out of nothing every day is endless. Here are some examples:

- Marketing campaigns
- New products and business lines
- Trusted partnerships with clients and customers
- Better processes and solutions to problems
- Job descriptions for new roles
- Employee policies, training curricula, performance management systems, and budgets (not to mention revenues)
- Thoughtful responses to customer complaints
- Names for the company softball team

Just about anyone who works in an organization is in the business of creating something out of nothing. The people who are able to create these somethings-out-of-nothing extraordinarily well approach the challenge with Yes, And. They may not call it that. They may call it extreme design or even conflict resolution. But in our world, it's called Yes, And, and it is the secret sauce, the source code, the key that unlocks every door worth opening. It is the foundational tenet of improvisation that allows all the other improv tenets to exist.

In the context of improvisation for the stage, where there is no script to guide the direction of a scene, Yes, And goes like this: One actor offers an idea onstage and other actors affirm and build onto that idea with something of their own.

Someone might say, for instance, "Wow, I've never seen so many stars in the sky."

The actor sharing the scene has only one responsibility at that point: to agree with this and add something new to it. So that could be something like, "I know. Things look so different up here on the moon."

That simple statement affirms what the first actor offered and added another idea (i.e., they're far away from the city—so far that they are actually on the moon). In turn, this affirmation gives the first actor some information to build on and opens up a great many possibilities for this scene.

If the second actor had negated the first actor's offering with something like, "I can't see a single star . . . it's broad daylight," the budding scene would have stopped in its tracks and left the first actor to scramble to find a response that could bring the scene back to speed in a way that an audience would find interesting. In our experience, audiences want to see something cool build onstage; they're not really interested in watching actors squabble over the essential facts of a scene—that's boring as hell.

Yes, And has a few synonyms in the improv world. You'll hear us talk about "affirming and building" on ideas or "exploring and heightening" a scene. There are variations, but the central idea of accepting what's offered and adding to it (regardless of what you may think of it) is absolutely foundational to everything we do at The Second City.

It's how we create scenes; it's how we develop rich, funny characters (think Wayne from "Wayne's World," created by Mike Myers originally on our stages, or Matt Foley, the dysfunctional motivational speaker that Chris Farley later made famous on *Saturday Night Live*), and it's core to how we develop entire shows. Yes, And leaves such an impression that alums like Tina Fey and Jane Lynch talk about it when they're writing memoirs or giving commencement speeches, long after they've left our stages. In fact, we'd say without hesitation that Yes, And is the lens through which we view our entire business and our place in the world. We are here to affirm and build upon people's ideas in a way that's smart, thoughtful, useful, interesting . . . and usually, uproariously funny.

—YES, BUT . . . HOW DOES IT RELATE TO BUSINESS?

For many of our corporate clients, Yes, And is a relatively easy concept to understand, but much harder to commit to in actual practice. That's because it requires you to trust others to support and build upon your contribution, and it requires you to do the same for them, whether you actually like the original idea or not. In the business world, support is almost always highly conditional: I'll support you as long as I understand immediately where this idea is going, or I'll support you as long as success is guaranteed, or I'll support you as long as there's something in it for me. "No" or "Yes, but" are popular in the work world because they allow one party to maintain control of an idea or conversation.

But if control guaranteed success in business, every business would be wildly successful, because most businesses place a premium on process, controls, models, and the like. We all know it's not that simple. Yes, And can often take you to unexpected places, and that makes some people nervous. But it's only when businesses let go a little and are willing to be surprised that they hit innovative gold.

We call this principle Yes, And because in our exercises, we preface each statement with those words. But it's the spirit of the principle that matters more than the words. To build a Yes, And culture, you have to model Yes, And behavior. You have to be supportive and committed to building on people's individual contributions.

USING YES, AND IN YOUR WORK

There is no Yes, And recipe book per se, but there are many situations and scenarios where a Yes, And mind-set can be helpful to individuals and organizations.

In Interpersonal and Team Communications

Let's go back to the case of our friend and client, Katie, the high-potential HR manager who had trepidation about assimilating into new teams. Katie felt especially shy about initiating conversations with new team members because she felt some self-imposed pressure in those situations to be a high-energy, life-of-the-party coworker. She thought that's what it meant to be a good networker and she didn't think her natural, more reserved personality would cut it in new team situations.

In the course of our work with Katie and her colleagues, we did a series of workshops that offered an improv model for communication that allowed Katie to be effective and comfortable. We had her perform another game called Doctor Know-It-All with two of her coworkers. They sat on the stage while the audience asked random questions, to which each of the three could reply using only one word at a time. We also played Take That Back, a game where people are prompted to change the last thing said, so that the scene onstage is ever changing and completely unpredictable, and the players have to scramble to adapt (as on a typical workday). We showed Katie that the best networkers are those who affirm and build on the ideas of others, not those who initiate and monopolize the conversation. Through fun, interactive exercises, she learned that the best way to connect and engage new colleagues is to listen deeply and build on their ideas, something that comes naturally when you're committed to a Yes, And approach to communication. Katie could see that her natural quiet style wasn't a deficiency. Rather it was in every way compatible with good networking and team building.

The best teams are made up of a variety of personality types with different styles, experiences, and strengths. As Katie gained the confidence to contribute to her group, her more assertive colleagues learned to give their more timid workmates space to contribute. They learned to encourage them to share their ideas rather than let them sit in silence on the sidelines. Katie was even able to get some pretty big laughs during her Doctor Know-It-All exercise because she was in full listening mode and made sense out of some pretty nonsensical situations. Her timing was perfect. After a half-day of exercises, you would never have pegged Katie as the shy one of the group. As long as she continued to practice and promote the concept of Yes, And she'd be a welcome member of any new team she joined in her high-potential job rotation.

In Coaching and Feedback Sessions

Good interpersonal communication is vital in business, among peers, but also between bosses and those who work for them. And if you're a boss, one of the most important responsibilities you have is to coach your people and provide feedback that will help them grow in their work. Yes, And is one of the best aids to improving interpersonal communications because of the three ways in which it can put everyday work communications in a more positive light.

First, Yes, And helps you acknowledge when someone does something good and gives you a chance to encourage that person to reach further. It also works well when people drop the ball, because it allows you to identify something redeemable about their work before commenting on mistakes or misjudgments, such as when the boss meets you after a particularly bad showing with,

"So we lost the account?" Yes, And allows you to respond truth-fully, but not passively: "Yes, and I think I know why. We'll break down what we did wrong this time so it won't happen again."

Second, adopting a Yes, And mind-set can be invaluable in motivating teams to reach for new heights when developing ideas and initiatives. During a collaborative leadership workshop with long-standing client Farmers Insurance, one of our more senior participants reflected elegantly on the challenge leaders sometimes face in staying open to ideas from their people, even when those ideas aren't new or intriguing at first blush: "Yes, And showed me that you're not going to love every idea, but it helps to love it for at least a little while." It's a terrific adage. Many of the franchises and products we have learned to love over the years didn't start so promisingly: *Seinfeld*, the brilliant sitcom from Larry David and Jerry Seinfeld, really did have its origins in a pitch meeting with the network as "a show about nothing"; J. K. Rowling was turned down by a number of publishers who didn't see how the boy wizard, Harry Potter, would ever capture anyone's imagination; and Tony Fadell, the inventor of the iPod, shopped around that idea to a few companies—all of whom re-jected the idea out of hand—before Steve Jobs said Yes, And. Sometimes you need to give the crazy idea in the room a second, third, and fourth look.

Finally, Yes And helps boss-subordinate communications by leveling the playing field of the conversation. By committing to listening and building on ideas, you tend to focus more on the merits of the idea, not the rank of the person who generated it. Dr. Hal M. Lewis, president and CEO of the Spertus Institute for Jewish Learning and Leadership, sees Yes, And as a vital leadership tool, saying, "Yes, And begins with the same funda-mental principle that's found in any classical understanding of leadership. Which is, none of us is as smart as all of us. As soon as I give up the notion that I have to be the smartest person in the room, magic can happen."[4]

Yes, And makes everyone feel heard and respected, and when you have mutual respect, it's possible to work through any performance challenge.

In Brainstorming and Ideation Sessions

Finding the new "new" always seems to be the Holy Grail in business, politics, sports, entertainment, and education. Our world puts a high premium on innovation, no matter your line of work. The evidence is all around us in the day-to-day language of life. Packaged goods companies tout "new and improved" laundry detergent. Political challengers stump about, talking about how they represent a "fresh change" from the tired ideas of incumbents. Educators extol the virtues of new technology in the classroom. And TV networks say odd things in their show promos, like, "Followed at eight by an all-new *Parks and Recreation*." (This always makes us wonder what a partially new *Parks and Rec* would be like. We love the show and think it would probably still be pretty cool.)

But for all the energy placed on creating new stuff, on innovating, there's a lot of sameness in the world, a lot of copycats, and a lot of innovation initiatives that end in failure (we may or may not be talking to you, One Direction).

And it's a real problem. According to an Ernst & Young study from 2010, only 47 percent of senior executives surveyed felt their companies were more innovative than their competition, 17 percent felt they were less innovative than the competition, and 41 percent felt they lacked big ideas to move their businesses forward.[5] There are several reasons for this. People might think that innovation and invention are someone else's responsibility, or they think that innovation is a separate discipline, a Skunk

Works, that needs to stand apart from day-to-day work activity. Usually, individuals and organizations struggle with innovation because it's hard to do consistently if you don't have an underlying philosophy that values creators and the process of innovation. We think the lack of innovation has more to do with the persistent presence of khakis in the workplace, but couldn't find any facts to support that observation.

So how can you boost innovation? By promoting Yes, And at every opportunity.

Probably the most obvious place you can apply Yes, And is in brainstorming or ideation sessions, where you and some teammates are trying to come up with a new product idea, marketing slogan, or creative theme. The creative process is actually similar to how we use Yes, And onstage. We've seen it work as an invaluable tool to help teams generate lots of ideas in a short period of time. In addition, we often see that it helps teams generate more unlikely or unusual ideas than they would in a traditional brainstorming approach. The reason is simple: When people are building and supporting each other's ideas quickly, they tend to filter and judge less, and when you take off filters at the early stage of a brainstorm session, you allow ideas to go to new places, and you discover new connections that conventional wisdom doesn't account for.

We are often brought in by clients to conduct innovation and creativity workshops at the start of a strategic planning process, at the kickoff of a new marketing campaign, or to set the stage for new and different ideas. In each case, we work hard to instill the Yes, And mentality into work teams. It's exactly this kind of commitment to Yes, And that led us to co-create a very successful marketing campaign with client Leggett & Platt, a company that makes . . . wait for it . . . the springs and coils that go into mattresses.

Let's face it, the mattress business isn't glamorous, and the spring and coil business even less so, but our clients at Leggett were creative folks, and in the course of one of our creative development brainstorms with them, we landed on the idea of creating a funny rap video that satirized rap video conventions and highlighted a key virtue of mattresses made with springs and coils: The sex is supposed to be better. Not only did the video we created drive huge buzz for their business, we were also able to help them change how the category viewed their products, all while creating a fun piece that everyone could be proud of. There are many instructive aspects of this assignment, but the key point is that we'd never have made the leap between springs and sexy rap video had we not Yes, Anded each other to find unlikely connections between seemingly disparate ideas.

In Problem Solving and Conflict Resolution

Let's face it. When the shit hits the fan at work and we've got unexpected problems to solve, we're often tempted to lock up and focus on the blame, repercussions, and grief we're going to feel from the higher-ups instead of focusing on solving the problem at hand. We experienced this firsthand in a crisis moment, which became a fantastic model for using Yes, And when things are looking pretty bleak.

One of our colleagues—to protect the various parties involved, we'll call him Jack—had just become board president for a high-profile cultural institution. Jack had been in the position for a total of two weeks when he received a call late on a Friday afternoon from the director. "It's an emergency. We need the whole board to meet us downtown right now." Once everyone arrived at the designated location, a private conference room at the company of one of the board members, the director spoke: "We have just discovered that a longtime employee of our organization, someone we have trusted as a colleague and a friend for many years, has been embezzling from the institution." As the details emerged, Jack was just as shocked as everyone else. Not only had someone they all trusted and liked completely betrayed that trust, but this individual had also left the institution in financial tatters. "We're broke, and we have to figure out how we're going to tell people and how we're going to rebuild for the future, or else this institution will cease to exist," said the director solemnly.

The next words Jack heard came from a rather well-known political consultant, a friend of the institution who had been called in to help. The mood in the room, which had been stunned silence, turned in a second when the consultant said, "There is a quote in my business that you learn to live by." He paused, then added, "Never let a good crisis go to waste."

Winston Churchill, the author of that quote, knew how to Yes, And.

The next three hours were an exercise in Yes, Anding their way through the crisis. The group needed to break the hard truth to its members. They debated how the message should be communicated and who would do it. Jack offered that, as the new board president, it should be his responsibility. The consultant added that since Jack was brand-new, he would be the perfect spokesperson in this crisis; he had been uninvolved in possible past transgressions inside the organization and would be able to engender trust and set a path moving forward. All communication would be transparent. Not only would Jack speak to the organization's members, the group would also create ongoing opportunities for conversation and informational updates each week for members, media, and sponsors.

As difficult as those days were for Jack and the institution, they survived, and they were eventually able to rebuild the financial sustainability of the organization. Without leadership in Yes, And mode, it's doubtful that would ever have happened.

Just as it is useful in extreme situations, Yes, And is useful in day-to-day decision making and problem solving with your co-workers. Often, problems repeat themselves, because the usual solutions we come up with aren't solving anything. In those situations, it's helpful to be able to enlist your coworkers to create new options and new solutions to these old problems. To achieve this, everyone needs to come from a place of Yes, And instead of No.

We like to say that when problem solving, even a bad idea is just a bridge to a better idea. Yes, And allows everyone to contemplate potentially useful but incomplete ideas before they get shut down. Creating a positive climate in the face of pressure and crises gives groups the confidence that they can solve whatever problem emerges. It happens all the time in our group huddles and executive meetings at The Second City. Like any business, we face our share of problems, but we tend to go into those problems with a can-do spirit because we have seen time and again that we will support each other until the problem is solved.

Our company's commitment to Yes, Anding our way through mayhem was never more apparent than in the fall of 2009. The Great Recession was wreaking the same havoc on our company as it was on so many others across the country, and we were feeling intense pressure to come up with some relief for our financial challenges. While the theatre business in Chicago remained steady, out-of-town tour dates and the almighty corporate dollar were diminishing rapidly. With the immediate economic future quite uncertain, the company went into belt-tightening mode. We put a hold on investments in new products and productions, we decreased the size of our touring ensembles, and we put a freeze on any new spending.

While we were laughing/crying our way through our financial crunch, an increasingly bizarre political melodrama was playing out in our city and state. Governor Rod Blagojevich, serving his second term in office, was under investigation for attempting to "sell" Illinois's seat in the U.S. Senate that had been vacated by President Barack Obama. Political horse-trading is one thing, but this investigation shone a light on the Blagojevich power structure that had all the comic riches of a Gilbert and Sullivan operetta. There was the powerful father-in-law who had been the Blagojevich puppet master, only to be spurned by the son-in-law when his services were no longer required; tapped phones revealed the governor's wife had a mouth like a sailor's; and the governor himself, holed up in his Northwest Side home in Chicago, spent more time jogging and brushing his hair than doing any actual governing.

It was at The Second City holiday party—after a few glasses of holiday punch—that a few of us, including Kelly, remarked on how theatrical this scandal was becoming. Off-handedly, Kelly said, "We should make a rock opera of the whole thing," which caught the ear of writer/performers Ed Furman and T. J. Shanoff, who were in conversation nearby. A few minutes later, Ed and TJ approached Kelly. "We figured out your rock opera," TJ offered. Then Ed added, "It's called *Rod Blagojevich Superstar.*"

Everyone laughed, and then stopped.

"You're serious, right?" asked Kelly.

"As a heart attack," said Ed.

But how were we going to mount a new production in the middle of a spending freeze?

Enter some serious Yes, And.

The next day, Kelly walked into Second City co-owner and executive producer Andrew Alexander's office.

"You know how we aren't supposed to add more projects or spend more money?" Kelly started. "Well, we were talking at the party last night . . . what if we rolled out a mini rock opera about the whole Blagojevich scandal? It's called *Rod Blagojevich Superstar*. The guys think they can write it pretty quickly."

Andrew paused maybe five seconds. "Yep. Go do that."

That was Yes, And number one.

Now we had to figure out the logistics of putting up a show on virtually no budget. "Can we find a free theatre space?"

"Yes, the e.t.c. space (our second stage in Chicago) is dark on Tuesdays and Wednesdays. We can play there."

"How do we pay people with no money?"

"We can get the writers and directors to work for a cut of the show's profits and we can call the actor's union to see if they will let us pay a little less to the actors in exchange for giving them a cut as well?"

"This governor could go to jail any minute. How quickly can we get the show written and rehearsed?"

"Will two weeks work?

Yes, And was in heavy rotation that day.

Ed and TJ were on board. We called the Actors' Equity Association. The great thing about a project like this is that when you mention the title, the person on the other end of the phone immediately laughs. With relatively little fuss, Actors' Equity provided Yes, And number four—saying that as long as the actors we used were in agreement, they would work with us to defer the larger fees associated with putting up a union show in exchange for a piece of the back end.

Some ideas were meant to happen. In our world, lightning strikes when the work you put onstage speaks directly to the zeitgeist. When we announced the show, the media pounced. By the time we were ready to put on our first preview performance, tickets for the entire run were sold out.

Walking into the theatre for that first preview, longtime local political reporter Carol Marin pointed out to us that an entire block of seats near the side of the stage was taken up by Blagojevich's staff members.

Needless to say, the show was a hit. Months later, we transferred the production to the Chicago Shakespeare Theatre on Navy Pier. Probably the ultimate Yes, And came when the disgraced governor himself joined us onstage for a performance. *Good Morning America* and FOX, MSNBC, and all the national networks covered the appearance. We created a second company that took the show on the road to downstate Illinois—home of the seat of Illinois government—where audiences howled at a show whose script was taken almost virtually word for word from the various press conferences and wiretap recordings that were flooding our news feeds every day as the scandal widened and grew. The show changed every night based on new information.

The show played for more than a year, and all the people who said Yes, And got to share in the economic success of a production that otherwise would never have happened.

Sometimes, just knowing that you can count on your colleagues for support makes all the difference in finding solutions to high-stakes problems.

In Overcoming Objections

In business, people spend a lot of time, money, and energy persuading each other to do stuff. Whether you're a salesperson closing a lunker deal, a consultant recommending a sweeping outsourcing program, or a marketing director fighting internally for a bigger budget, you know how hard it can be to get the person on the other side of the desk to go along with you. In any high-stakes decision, people are bound to have objections. You want to do everything possible to avoid creating an adversarial atmosphere. Keeping a Yes, And perspective in these situations can help you validate the legitimate concerns of the other party and keep the door open for common ground.

We've seen clients lose out on a deal or recommendation not because the facts weren't on their side, but because they failed to create the environment of trust that is key to any new agreement or partnership. This was true for a renowned management consulting firm that brought Second City Works in to help them address feedback they'd gotten from clients that suggested the firm came across as arrogant and condescending. Clients respected and valued the analysis and recommendations they got from the firm, but had a hard time separating that from the unpleasant interactions they had with the company's consultants. As a consequence, the firm was missing out on additional business from its clients, who wanted their experience to be more collaborative and less confrontational.

First, we had to find a way to help the consultants see where they were going wrong without putting them on the defensive. No one likes to be told they're arrogant. We were able to help the consulting firm in a couple of ways. For example, we created funny vignettes to satirize typical interactions from the client's perspective, such as the human interrupter—a character we created who would not let any other individual finish a sentence or even express a full thought. That one got a particularly rousing response by showing how the consultants prized being right more than connecting with clients. Then we conducted a series of workshops to help the consultants improve their listening skills, with an emphasis on creating a more positive tone, even when they were conveying difficult news or making tough recommendations.

In this case, as in most, Yes, And was the central idea supporting our work with the client. It wasn't just about teaching them to utter those words specifically, though. More important, we encouraged them to communicate generously and collaboratively, and to look for ways to reach agreement, which is ultimately what is needed to make anything happen in business.

For us at The Second City, innovation is part of the day-to-day ethic in the building—to improvise is to innovate. While some of our inventiveness comes from the people we hire, who are inherently creative, it's actually more than that. We choose to align ourselves around a specific Yes, And philosophy that leads us to a consistently great creative product, an expanding business and an ever-growing pool of like-minded talent who lead us into even more invention.

YES, AND, BEYOND THE OBVIOUS

The previous examples show how Yes, And can work as a management tool, but Yes, And influences the business world in less overt ways, too. In fact, we'd argue that improv ideas like Yes, And are alive and well all around us, every day. We just don't recognize them as such.

Don't believe us?

Two examples of Yes, And operating in the tech world are Wikipedia, the online encyclopedia, and Linux, the open-source operating system that has gained great traction in technology over the past couple decades.

Many of you probably have some experience with Wikipedia, especially if you have a teenager who is working on a term paper that is three days late. Content is user generated, meaning anyone can create, edit, or add to content that is already written, whether the topic is radio waves or Radiohead. As with Yes, And on the stage, Wikipedia operates on what we call an Explore and Heighten model, meaning something is offered, then built upon, deepened, and sometimes even redirected. Explore and Heighten is the improvisation tenet that comes after Yes, And. Once you've learned how to build together, Explore and Heighten lets you build something of interest and weight. It's great to begin with a positive, but the path to success invariably comes when we go deeper. And even though this approach can lead to crazy Wiki entries and dodgy term papers, the strength of the underlying idea—Yes, Anding something that was offered by someone else—is readily apparent.

Another good example is Linux, which (according to Wikipedia!) is a Unix-like operating system assembled under the model of free and open-source software development and distribution.[6] Now, we don't know Jack about software development, and we won't try to fake it, but we see this as another under-the-radar example of Yes, And in action. Developers can use and modify existing code and make it do cool new things . . . and they have. Linux is now the leading OS for servers and mainframes, and more than 90 percent of the world's fastest supercomputers run some version of Linux. And just think, all this started with the Linux kernel, an operating system first developed in 1991 by Linus Torvalds. Thank you, Linus, for your brilliant initiation. Thank you, developers all over the world, for Yes, Anding Linus and creating such a useful system. In essence, you could say that Linux is the most powerful, benevolent, and useful expression of Yes, And the world has ever seen. Take a bow, Linus and friends. You're world-class improvisers and you didn't even know it.

Yes, And as Ensemble Maker and Mistake Eraser

There are some things to keep in mind as you go about applying Yes, And to your daily work.

Think about it. If you are Yes, Anding your way through a brainstorm or conversation in a typical work or social environment, your role is to support the ideas of others as often as you initiate ideas of your own. That can be hard, even for someone who believes in the power of Yes, And. Supporting actors are hugely important in business, but they're not as valued as they should be in a culture that favors the rock star CEO, the billionaire VC, the larger-than-life entrepreneur, and stars and celebrities in general. It's funny, in the old days celebrity was reserved for Hollywood stars and sports heroes. Now, in our 24/7 media culture, everyone gets a chance at his or her fifteen minutes, thanks to shows like *Undercover Boss*, *Shark Tank*, and all the business news shows on cable TV. Clearly, Andy Warhol was right.

In this world, it's tempting to go it alone and aspire to hero status. That's what seems to be rewarded most visibly, especially in the movies. It's harder to remember the value of affirming and building on the ideas of others. But it's also far more practical. Yes, And builds better ensembles, which, in turn, make stars of everyone on the stage and in the workplace, as we'll explore further in the next chapter.

If you've ever struggled against inertia or you keep making false starts, take hope in this: Most grand ideas don't start grand, and many of the best inventions come from happy accidents and thoughtful pivots off mistakes.

- The pacemaker was initially supposed to be a device that lowered body temperature through use of a radio frequency.
- The Slinky was supposed to be a machinery part for a battleship (and where would we be without the Slinky?).
- Fireworks, legend has it, were the result of a kitchen experiment gone wrong.

Great improvisers know how to roll with miscues and goof ups. We are the ultimate lemonade makers. Mistakes can cause stress in the moment, but they also provide inspiration to new thinking and new possibilities if you're coming from a Yes, And mind-set. We say, "Make accidents work." These examples show the awesome potential of that approach if you can get beyond your fear of failure.

Yes, And Affirms and Builds

The beauty of Yes, And lies in the incremental way it allows ensembles to build one big, solid idea out of a multitude of smaller ones. We have developed an axiom at The Second City to explain to new actors and clients how we want them to approach idea generation: Bring a brick, not a cathedral. Sometimes an improviser will fall in love with one fully formed idea before a scene has had a chance to develop and force that idea on his ensemble mates, even when it doesn't make sense. He'll "bring a cathedral" to the scene when all the group really needs is another brick. A cathedral stops all creative movement short; bricks allow the innovative process to flourish.

We do an exercise in the beginning levels of our Training Center to illustrate the power of this idea. It's called One-Word Story and it goes like this: People gather in circles, usually of six to ten, and are asked to tell an original story. Each person is allowed to contribute only one word at a time toward the overall narrative. This is tough for many people, especially creative people used to working in their own silos, because they tend to get inspired or they want to control where the story is going. But they can't, because they can add only the most logical next word in the story when it comes to their turn. If you are a big brain in the room, you want to be able to use that impressive vocabulary. Indeed, sometimes the most logical word is big, unusual, and polysyllabic (e.g., rhinoceros). But sometimes the only logical word to contribute is *and*. It's a great exercise for Type A personalities to remember that each of us, at some point, has to play a supporting part—we can't always be the star pupil. The exercise plays out over several minutes, and, as you might imagine, a story developed this way takes hilarious and unexpected twists and turns. Individual participants affirm and build in their unique way to a far more interesting story than they probably would have come up with on their own.

Some people really struggle with the exercise. Many of us have the tendency to want to bring the big idea—the fully built cathedral—ourselves, probably so we can get all the credit. During the One-Word Story, these people will engage in all sorts of inadvertent power plays and control grabs. They'll break the rules of the game by offering full phrases instead of single words to shape the story; they'll ignore the words that come before theirs and jam their own idea in whether or not it makes sense; they'll criticize other people's contributions when they don't like the direction the story is going in, and so on.

Sound familiar? It's not a stretch to see parallel behaviors in our own organizations. People get an idea and by fixating on it, fail to seek the contributions of others. Sometimes great ideas emerge from this approach, but, more often, those initial ideas never fulfill their potential. When this happens in our workshops, the first thing we do is get these individuals to play the game by the rules by appealing to their intellect, their vanity, and their desire to get things right. Then we reinforce the lesson that the game teaches: We are all part of this storytelling, and the most creative of us, the most lone wolf, can continue to make important contributions even if he or she concedes to play a smaller part in the process. It's a message leaders should share with their organizations more often.

What does the exercise teach us? First, that every contribution matters, even seemingly small ones. Too often, businesses give that idea only lip service. The ones that don't, however—the ones that fully commit to Yes, And—see their rates of successful innovation soar. You can get a lot more done in a lot less time when your ensemble works together to build a cathedral instead of waiting around for one individual at a time to do it.

Second, because every contribution matters, everyone has to engage and contribute. They can't opt out or tune out, because they'll hold the overall group back if they do. This exercise makes it clear to everyone, no matter how bold and brash or quiet and reserved, that they need to bring their best contributions or the group will suffer.

Last, this exercise gives people a safe way to practice ceding control to the group and illustrates how breakthroughs happen when people stop trying to control every outcome. In this exercise and in business, there is truth in the idea that "all of us are better than any of us."

WHAT YES, AND ISN'T

Obviously, we're true believers in Yes, And; you could even say that our entire fifty-five-year history is a living, breathing example of Yes, And in action. Our growth has really been all about affirming and building upon what works. Where we started with a single stage, we've evolved into a multifaceted entertainment and education organization that has gone beyond its Chicago roots to stretch around the globe. It's gotten to the point where we use Yes, And as a verb. We'll Yes, And our coworkers' ideas in meetings, and we'll Yes, And our way into new real estate, business ventures, partnerships, and programs.

It Isn't a Substitute for No

But even we know that there is a time and place for Yes, And. In our public and private workshops, there is the inevitable moment when an individual registers her overwhelming cynicism toward the practicality of instituting a Yes, And approach inside a business culture. "But seriously, not every idea is a good idea," she offers. "How can we do our jobs in any sort of productive way if we're mired in supporting bad ideas?"

We'd never suggest that people or companies should just say yes to every idea they come across. We're in the comedy business, but even we have some limits. There are times when people have to be told no. There are even times when Yes, And can be manipulative and counterproductive.

It Isn't a Replacement for Discretion, Quality, or Even Common Sense

Yes, And is simply the best way to approach the beginning stages of ideation. It's a way to allow individuals and groups to bring their best selves and, in turn, their best ideas to the room.

Just as players toss a baseball around on the field before playing an actual game, brainstorming requires the same warm-up for the part of our brain that's looking for a spark of creativity. Installing a Yes, And approach at the beginning of a creative session primes the pump for a conversation in motion.

You parse, dissect, and, as often as not, throw ideas away. But not until they have been heard.

It Isn't Always Used for Good

There are plenty of people so mastered in the art of saying no that they disguise it as saying "Yes, And." In the 1997 revue *Paradigm Lost*, Tina Fey and Scott Adsit created a scene that illustrates that particular manipulation perfectly. In her time at

The Second City, Tina was nothing if not a keen observer of gender bias and politics. In this particular scene, Tina and Scott play professors who are meeting for the first time in preparation for a collaborative project. Tina is grading papers as Scott enters:

> **ADSIT** Student paper?
> **FEY** Yes.
> **ADSIT** What's the subject?
> **FEY** Kevorkian.
> **ADSIT** Oh, Kevorkian. Dr. Death. What a monster. He should be put away forever, don't you think?
> **FEY** Oh, you don't like Kevorkian, huh?
> **ADSIT** Oh, horrible man. Murderer.

At this point, Scott's professor has clearly laid down the gauntlet. He morally objects to the work of Dr. Jack Kevorkian and physician-assisted suicide.

> **FEY** Well, I think the jury nullification of his cases indicates that there is a gray area there.
> **ADSIT** Really?
> **FEY** There's an ethical question being posed that our current laws don't account for. I mean, have you seen these people he assists? Their bodies are ravaged by pain, but their minds are completely lucid.

In response to Scott's character, Tina clearly disagrees—she adopts the opposite position on the matter of Kevorkian. Now watch how Scott's professor manipulates Tina's character's position to become his own.

ADSIT Well, they're in terrible pain, obviously. But these people are at the end of their lives, they don't want some stranger coming in and sitting at their bedside and telling them whether they should live or die.

FEY No, they want to make that decision themselves.

ADSIT Exactly. That's my point. They should be able to make that decision. If they want to die, they should be allowed to die. I'm just glad there's someone like Kevorkian who's willing to do it. I'm surprised he even went to trial.

FEY So we actually agree?

ADSIT No. I support Kevorkian.

As a nod to the target of their satire, Tina and Scott titled this scene "Yes, And."

The enemies of Yes, And are not always the loudest no in the room. Often, they are saying yes with their mouths while saying no with their actions. Just to keep things honest, we at The Second City have been just as vulnerable to these phenomena as those in any other business. A quick survey of our producing team at The Second City provided these moments of anti–Yes, And behavior inside the hallowed halls of the mecca of improvisation:

- Getting to No by Numbers: If you're the top dog and your team comes to a consensus but it's not to your liking, just add more and more voices to the room until you get the no you were looking for.
- Yes, And I'm Overstepping My Role: Yes, And can be a wonderful refuge if you want to stick your nose into other departments when you were never invited to do so. Yes, And becomes a very useful tool to

insert yourself into an area in which you are both unskilled and unwanted by simply proclaiming that you are Yes, Anding.

- Yes, And . . . Go Hang Yourself: Sometimes you can see when people's actions are clearly going to bring them to the brink of disaster. If you don't like them, simply Yes, And their idea. That way, you can ruin them without ever being blamed for not being a team player.
- No, but Yes, And It's Mine: How about when someone says no emphatically to an idea, only to adopt the same idea and collect the accolades for their brilliant thinking.
- Yes, And They Will Forget They Ever Brought This Up: Sometimes you just say Yes, And to shut people up for the moment, fully knowing that they will eventually forget they brought up the idea in the first place. It's a great tactic to avoid saying no.
- The Power in Saying Neither No or Yes: Maintain your power by never taking a stand on anything. No one can say you made a bad decision when you never make any decision at all.

In sum, there will always be reasons to say no, just as there will be individuals whom we interact with in our work lives who present ongoing challenges to a Yes, And model. Kick off your brainstorming with a reminder of how you want to Yes, And; give teams an opportunity to practice their Yes, Anding; and use all the tools at your disposal—language, physical cues, humor—to model inclusivity and make clear you expect others to make room for ideas other than their own.

In our experience with corporate clients, no is too often the default answer, and it's offered reflexively as a way to avoid risk and the possibility of failure. That's understandable, but it also exacts a high cost in the form of ideas that are never offered, new approaches that are shut down before they have a chance, and teams that never reach their potential because people hold back. It may be hard actually to quantify the adverse impacts of a no culture, but it comes out in lots of ways, including high customer dissatisfaction and a loss of employee engagement in their work and their companies.

What we're really saying in the end is that no cannot be your default response if you want to create a work environment that is fast, innovative, supportive, and high functioning over time. Yes, And gives the world pace, energy, and forward momentum. And it gives the people who practice it the confidence that, come what may, in business or their personal lives, they can create something out of nothing and make something wonderful out of it.

HOW TO BUILD AN
ENSEMBLE

There is a lot of talk in business about building teams, and we offer a variety of team-building courses that seek to strengthen an individual's role within the larger group, thereby improving the group as a whole. But the word we use at The Second City when we talk about the people engaged in the act of creativity is *ensemble*. These definitions can give you a sense of the subtle difference:

TEAM: A number of persons forming one of the sides in a game or contest.

ENSEMBLE: All the parts of a thing taken together, so that each part is considered only in relation to the whole.[7]

The word *team* implies competition, which inherently suggests some external foe that the group is working against. *Ensemble* carries no such baggage; it is a thing unto itself, an entity that is only its true self when its members are performing as one.

Teams have starters and bench players; there is an absolute hierarchy in play that any parent of the twelfth man on a high school basketball team can tell you conveys a clear message that some of the team members matter and some simply do not. Ensembles, on the other hand, may have a first chair, second chair, and third chair, but all those chairs are on the stage and they play in almost every movement.

At The Second City, we believe in building ensembles, not teams. The high-functioning ensemble is a gift to both management and the workforce. Supervisors and managers get the benefit of a finely tuned unit, capable of generating and executing ideas autonomously, yet also in sync with the business as a whole. Individuals benefit because they get better by engaging with folks who are as good as or better than they are. An ensemble lifts you in direct relation to the diverse skill sets of those you are working with. Just look at the history of our company: an ensemble theatre that has developed the careers of more comic stars in the last five decades than any other theatrical institution.

To put it simply, stars are born out of ensembles—without ever sacrificing the greater needs of the whole group.

Let us be clear that we're not altogether against the word *team*. In fact, we use that word a lot to describe the functions of the various groups that make up our business and many of the businesses we work with. But the word does not imply the depth and shared accountability that comes with a high-functioning ensemble.

In this chapter we will explain why it's so important to build ensembles throughout your business. We will look at some specific examples of ensemble building, how we do it at The Second City, and how we've translated our methodologies to a variety of other businesses. We'll examine what kind of individual DNA makes for the best ensembles and explore some of the barriers that can hinder their coalescence. And since we know that not every company has the ability to build ensembles from scratch, we'll give you some specific exercises that you can bring to your current teams to help you begin to turn them into ensembles.

REASONS TO BUILD AN ENSEMBLE

Let's start with this: *Successful solo acts are rarely, in fact, solo.* It's a fantastic American myth—the individual entrepreneur whose single-minded vision is scorned and laughed at until he prevails through sheer determination, often to the detriment of friends, family, and anyone else who did not fall in line behind the visionary. It makes for a great movie, but it has never been the whole story. From Ford to Jobs, a litany of simplified success stories exist that exclude the legions of fellow creatives and noncreatives alike who contributed to the overall success of the endeavor.

Unless you're swimming in an individual race, chances are that your job will rely on your ability to interact successfully with a variety of other individuals, some of whom you may have handpicked, but the vast majority of whom you will have been engaged with by means of entropy.

So your day-to-day working life is a near-constant act of engagement with other individuals. But when you are called on to innovate, you need to take that engagement to the next level. When any business is tasked with a major initiative, it forms task forces and teams because its staff knows the success of the endeavor can be assured only if groups of people work in synchronicity to achieve the goal.

Ensembles in the form of collaborations, mash-ups, and

partnerships have become a powerful force in the world of innovation from Silicon Valley to SoHo. In Chicago, Eric Lefkofsky and Brad Keywell's company Lightbank is on the cutting edge of venture capitalism, creating a business ecosystem for technology start-ups focused on disruptive technology. Just walking through their offices on the banks of the Chicago River, you see a variety of companies, such as Belly, Locu, Qwiki, and Hipster, sharing physical space and resources. Thanks to this creative arrangement, best practices are shared quickly and the proximity of talent pools fuels unexpected results every day. Lefkofsky and Keywell created an ensemble by proximity. They bet on the fact that creative individuals from different fields could benefit by working side by side over a period of time, and that the shared space would promote interactions that may have started casually, but might lead to new discoveries and initiatives.

Collaborations Can Create Synergy

In the arts, Elvis Costello has found that his collaborative albums often outsell his solo records; great modern choreographers from Alvin Ailey to Twyla Tharp have developed their pieces with the input—often improvised—of their dancers. The smash Broadway hit *The Drowsy Chaperone* began life as a wedding present from some Toronto writer/performers to Second City alums Bob Martin and Janet Van de Graaf in 1997. That group decided to take the "present" and turn it into a show at the Toronto Fringe Festival. The legendary Mirvish producing team in Toronto joined forces with the creatives to give the show a broader commercial run at the 160-seat Theatre Passe Muraille in Toronto, and then a bigger production at the 1,000-seat Winter Garden Theatre in New York City. Adding some Broadway producers to the mix, *The Drowsy Chaperone* made its Broadway debut in 2006, going on to win the Tony Award for Best Musical.

But for every successful collaboration, you have an AOL–Time Warner or an Oasis. Looking back, AOL–Time Warner was never a true collaboration of equals. At the time of the merger, AOL's worth was approximately twice that of Time Warner, but they had only about half the cash flow. And folks on the inside said that the two cultures never meshed. As for English rock band Oasis, sometimes brothers just don't get along.

Building a great ensemble allows you to take individual differences—even divergent points of view—and incorporate them in such a complementary way that the ensemble functions even better together than the individuals do on their own. The rapid exchange of ideas between talented individuals fuels creativity and innovation. Further, when building an ensemble of talent, you are setting the groundwork for your organization's survival and growth.

Ensembles Preserve Talent

Years ago, we were visited by executives from The Onion, the legendary satiric media company that recently moved its headquarters from New York to Chicago. The conversation turned toward the topic of retaining talent. "How do you keep your talent?" they asked. "We don't," we replied.

At The Second City, we develop young comic voices, often giving them their first professional work on a union stage. It is inevitable that they will leave. The genius of this company—an approach set up long before we joined the business—was to create a system that was continually able to refresh its creative force. Each generation of artists teaches our improvisational methodologies to the next. When one actor from our resident stage leaves, it opens the door for the next of comedy's best and brightest. This revolving door of talent has taught us that an ensemble isn't one specific group of individuals. At The Second City, ensemble is simply the group mechanism. Each ensemble is unique and every time a new member is lost or added, a new ensemble forms. When we are at our best, we embrace each new ensemble and celebrate how it works differently from the previous one. We pay attention to what the previous ensemble member brought to the group but, most important, we don't try to duplicate those skills. Instead, we value the contributions of the new member and allow for the ensemble to be changed.

Developing ensembles within your company will give you a distinct advantage. Rather than being forced to rely on one creative voice to guide the entire organization, you create a chorus of creative voices who have skin in the game, who feel responsible and take it upon themselves to protect, sustain, and grow the business. They also become well equipped to welcome new creatives over time. In addition, creating ensembles where everyone carries the weight, feels important, and is encouraged to contribute will actually slow down the talent drain. Talent will always be drawn to bigger and better opportunities, so shouldn't you be providing them ample chance to become part of something bigger than themselves?

Only in a high-functioning ensemble can you continually weave talent in and out. And our ensembles have been doing this since December 16, 1959, never closing and always adapting new voices into the mix.

ENSEMBLE WORK IS REALLY HARD . . . BUT IT'S WORTH THE EFFORT

The bigger your organization, the harder it will be to maintain a cohesive ensemble. Most people in business don't set out to create a network of isolated silos, but they come to learn that the more people they involve in any large endeavor, the slower, more cumbersome, and more complicated that endeavor becomes.

In response to that reality, people struggling with big projects usually do what most rational people do: They keep their efforts close at hand and their spheres of approval small. We've heard this called the Saving Private Ryan effect, where people ultimately save their best efforts for the small circle of people closest to them. In the case of the movie, the soldiers sent out to find and rescue Private Ryan ultimately fought and died for each other, not for the more abstract ideas of freedom and democracy. In war or in big companies, the easiest, most natural response to complexity is to avoid unnecessary collaboration that will make things harder or riskier than they have to be.

But as challenging as collaboration can be, we know from experience that tight-knit, high-functioning ensembles can create things that no individual could do on his own.

We see it happen every day on our stages. Our process for creating content through an ensemble approach has allowed us to maintain a steady stream of productions for more than five decades. Additionally, we have been able to translate this expertise across a variety of platforms, using our ensemble approach to help teachers engage more productively with their students, to aid not-for-profit leaders in their quest to build community buy-in for their efforts, and in business to light the creative spark in groups of coworkers who have otherwise been left to work together with little or no direction.

A recent engagement with a global medical device company illustrates how our approach to talent management and development can be applied to domains that, on the surface, look far different from ours. We worked with one particular product team at this company that faced significant, even daunting challenges. The team is global, with the bulk of employees working out of

U.S. and U.K. offices. They wanted to establish stronger connections between their regional offices, despite time zone and cultural differences. They work in a highly regulated medical device business category, yet they wanted to encourage their people to be more creative thinkers. They wanted to empower their teams to make decisions locally, but they also needed to help them manage conflict effectively so they could get alignment and make progress even in situations where consensus was hard to reach.

Over a number of engagements, we created a workshop series to help them communicate more openly in a way that transcended cultural differences and formed a more cohesive ensemble. We also showed them how to create an environment that encouraged and supported people to offer creative solutions to long-standing problems. In such a series of workshops, we'll do literally dozens of improv exercises and follow up each exercise with a facilitator debrief to link the exercise to real-world application. Second City Training Center co-founder Sheldon Patinkin often notes that the brilliance of the improv games is that just playing them together creates ensembles.

One effective exercise we tried is called Talk Without I. As its name implies, it involves pairing up participants to have a conversation where they can't use the word *I*. As is customary in our workshops, we let the participants have conversations about anything; this helps them focus on speaking without *I* instead of focusing on a work-related conversation, which we've found can get people sidetracked from the point of the exercise. Talk Without I helps people recognize how they filter information through their own perspectives when sharing ideas, feedback, or recommendations. And in doing this, people learn to frame things in a way that is more accessible and understandable to their ensemble mates, thereby showing greater empathy, which often invites greater participation from colleagues, or at least minimizes conflict when there are disagreements. It's a fun way of teaching people the value of being other-directed. After running the exercise, we talk about what it took to be successful to complete it and how people can be more conscious of their own point of view when sharing ideas or evaluating the recommendations of others. As F. Scott Fitzgerald wrote, "The test of a first-rate intelligence is the ability to hold two opposed ideas in mind at the same time and still maintain the ability to function."[8] Effective individuals at work inside an ensemble constantly play with this dynamic. On the one hand, they demand that their ideas be listened to; on the other, they are keenly aware that their idea—no matter how brilliant—can be acted on only when embraced by others.

Other prime attributes of successful ensemble members include the ability to exist and operate in the moment; master the roles of give and take; and surrender the need always to be right. But it starts with casting. Or, in your case, you might call it hiring.

The first thing you have to understand is that it isn't easy. As longtime Second City director Jeff Richmond once wrote in a hastily scribbled note left on a producer's desk after a particularly ugly improvisational session: "This is the most inefficient way to create art! Ever!"

Here's why: In a group, you are susceptible to each individual's mood and baggage, emotional or otherwise. You need to build and maintain consensus, you need to be constantly aware of how the group dynamic is affecting the individuals in the group, and you must be aware of how the individuals affect the group. People are complicated, so ensembles are, too.

Ensembles must constantly shift in reaction to changing group dynamics. In scripted theatre, a director gives direction to the individual actor from a play whose words don't change, although the subtext may be open to interpretation. In business, careers often start with the same dynamic. We are handed a script (or a job description) to follow and if we do so, we can continue to collect our paycheck each week. But moving up the ranks in any business means that you are no longer relying on someone else's script; more often than not, you're supposed to be writing your own script—as well as the script for others. Everyone has to be flexible for ensembles to work.

You can see examples of this kind of flexible ensemble work in sports, too. Think of the great Chicago Bulls teams of the 1990s flying down the court—Jordan to Pippen to Jordan to Kerr—relying on instinct grounded in practice and repetition. But more important, their success was realized when the great individuals of that team surrendered some of their individual glory to play the game as an ensemble. Jordan, perhaps the greatest basketball player in the history of the game, played seven seasons before winning an NBA championship. His work ethic was unmatched; he would practice the simple art of free throws long after the rest of the team had gone home. But it wasn't until coach Phil Jackson convinced his superstar to buy into his improvisational game plan that the Chicago Bulls ran off six world championships. As Jackson himself noted: "Basketball, unlike football with its prescribed routes, is an improvisational game, similar to jazz. If someone drops a note, someone else must step into the vacuum and drive the beat that sustains the team."[9]

In the business world, corporate leaders are learning that it's the ensemble that moves the needle. In a 2009 interview with the *New York Times*, Darden Restaurant CEO Clarence Otis Jr. talked about his background in theatre when noting the importance of the ensemble: "It's less and less about getting the work done and more and more about building the team—getting the right people in place who have the talent and capability to get the work done and letting them do it."[10]

The foundation for a great ensemble starts with the talent. Jeff Richmond's moment of frustration aside (he went on to help produce one of the great ensemble-based television comedies of all time, *30 Rock*), when the ensemble is finally working in perfect unison, the results are magical.

HOW TO BUILD A GREAT ENSEMBLE

People love lists. They are easy to comprehend and they tell a story without any narrative around them. How's this for a list: Mike Nichols; Elaine May; Ed Asner; Shelley Berman; Jerry Stiller; Anne Meara; Alan Arkin; Barbara Harris; Severn Darden; Fred Willard; Joan Rivers; Robert Klein; Alan Alda; David Steinberg; Valerie Harper; Linda Lavin; Dick Schaal; Peter Boyle; Dan Aykroyd; John Belushi; Gilda Radner; Bill Murray; John Candy; Catherine O'Hara; Martin Short; Eugene Levy; Harold Ramis; Dave Thomas; Andrea Martin; Joe Flaherty; Betty Thomas; Jim Belushi; Tim Kazurinsky; Shelley Long; George Wendt; Bonnie Hunt; Mike Myers; Ryan Stiles; Dan Castellaneta; Richard Kind; Colin Mochrie; Julia Louis-Dreyfus; Jane Lynch; Bob Odenkirk; Jeremy Piven; Chris Farley; Tim Meadows; Adam McKay; Steve Carell; David Koechner; Stephen Colbert; Amy Sedaris; Rachel Dratch; Horatio Sanz; Tina Fey; Amy Poehler; Keegan-Michael Key; Jason Sudeikis; Aidy Bryant; Cecily Strong.

Every one of these individuals logged hours in The Second City system, either as a member of our predecessor, The Compass Players, or in touring ensembles or resident stages. Generation after generation of top-tier comedy talent has received its career training at the same institution. Clearly, something is working.

And although it's far more fun to mythologize the unbelievable track record we have amassed for launching the careers of so many great artists over so many years, the reality is that in building a school and professional stage that has become so established, we have an unseemly wealth of talent from which to choose. The list of folks who never actually made it onto one of our professional resident stages after studying with us is almost equally august, as it includes such notable stars as Keanu Reeves, Halle Berry, Jon Favreau, Kate Walsh, Kristen Schaal, Craig Robinson, Eric Stonestreet, and almost the entire Kids in the Hall ensemble.

Our approach to hiring may be simple, but it's not without nuance. Just as you wouldn't field a baseball team with nine right-handed sluggers, a stage ensemble is made up of players who make the whole greater through the diversity of their skills and personalities. So to build a great ensemble, we look for a variety of individuals who each possess strengths that will be enhanced within the group, and whose weaknesses will be minimized by it. Businesses must do the same. A manager's ability to identify the key talents of his employees—whether C-level, middle management, or operational—is paramount to fashioning a high-functioning ensemble.

It's not just about hiring to provide the business with a variety of expertise, either. It's really quite simple. Like-minded individuals from like-minded backgrounds will produce like-minded results. But the world we live in today demands that we challenge the status quo; it demands a diversity of approaches to real-world problems. It's about gathering a diversity of voices and life experiences to fuel the creative fires of innovation.

In other words, hiring well often means hiring different.

"If it ain't broke, don't fix it." It's an adage that is often true, but not always wise. We learned this the hard way at The Second City. By the 1970s and through the '80s, our ensemble had begun to take on a somewhat predictable pattern. There was the straight man, the funny fat guy, the ingenue—add a character actor and actress and you had a classic Second City cast. *The Simpsons* famously took a shot at us when Homer visited Chicago in a 2007 episode. The animated sign hanging in front of our famous arches on Wells Street read, "See Great Comedians Before They Get Fat."[11]

Through the first three decades of our existence, our casts in Chicago were almost all male, Caucasian, and straight. We share that dubious distinction with a vast number of American businesses.

When your product is selling and your clients are happy, it's easy to rest on your laurels and to become complacent. Many people find it easier to take great risks when the chips are down and they have nothing to lose. But success should also provide you the opportunity for introspection. Innovators don't stop at good, and improvisers are restless creatives for whom risk is the ultimate aphrodisiac. Our prototypical casting came about from a kind of malaise that was actually born out of our success.

Andrew Alexander never understood the cause of the gender imbalance at The Second City in Chicago. In Canada, where he ran the Toronto operation along with the classic *SCTV* television series in the 1970s and 1980s, the casts were almost always gender equal. Ultimately, he threw down the gauntlet—all Second City casts would be equal parts men and women. First, each touring company was made gender equal, and in the following years the Second City Mainstage and Second City e.t.c. companies would become gender equal.

Tina Fey was part of the first gender-equal cast at The Second City Chicago in the 1996 Mainstage revue *Citizen Gates*. Another member of that cast was Tina's future *Saturday Night Live* cast mate Rachel Dratch. The third female ensemble member, Jenna Jolovitz, went on to write for *Mad TV*.

Today, more women take classes at The Second City Training Center than men, a fact that we believe is due in no small part to the years in which the women on our stages were equal in numbers to the men. The same, however, cannot be said for actors of color.

The year that Kelly started producing for The Second City, 1992, was also the year that Andrew created The Second City Outreach Program, an initiative designed to increase diversity in our school and on our stages. The origins of the Outreach Program go back to a warm night in late April. Andrew happened to be scheduled to fly from Los Angeles to Chicago on April 29, 1992, the day the Los Angeles race riots began in the wake of the Rodney King verdict. As the plane ascended, he could see smoke billowing from the streets below. It was an arresting image. When Andrew landed in Chicago, thousands of miles away from the melee that engulfed Los Angeles, he headed over to The Second City Mainstage, arriving in time for the third act of the evening—the improvised set. When a cast is in rehearsal, the Improv Set is used to test out new material. When we are not in rehearsal, more often than not the cast improvises based on the news of the day. Naturally, that night the first audience suggestion was the race riots. And being the good improvisers that they were, the cast took that suggestion and valiantly attempted to use improvised humor as a way to talk about the tragedy that was unfolding simultaneously on the West Coast. There was one significant problem: The cast was all white.

The stage was set: talented, earnest, funny white people looking to find truth and profundity in comic improvisation with other white people. That mix was going to provide neither cast nor audience members with any significant insights on this issue.

The next day, Andrew called Kelly and the rest of the management team into his office. "What will it take to make our casts more diverse?" he asked. The answers included "getting more actors of color into our classes" and "welcoming diverse voices into our building and onto our stages," and finally, "making the hiring of diverse talent a priority throughout the company." So we did. That summer, The Second City Outreach Program hosted three local comedy troupes at a series of workshops and performances: the Latin-American troupe Salsation; the Asian-American troupe Stir Friday Night; and a group of LGBT performers that Second City helped create called Gay Co. Scholarships were created so that young actors of color could take classes at The Second City free of charge. Most vitally, when hiring for the professional companies, diversity was put on the list of the most important attributes to consider.

There's really nothing like watching a bunch of white liberals faced with confronting true integration in their own backyard. Not everyone was comfortable with Andrew's plan. Everyone championed his idea in theory, but then some lost their enthusiasm when they realized it was going to affect their actual day-to-day job. The most common concern expressed was that The Second City should always hire the absolute "best" improvisers for their ensembles, and by focusing on gender or diversity we might sacrifice quality.

But this concern ignored the underlying principles that define the best ensembles. The best should be defined by how they work as a group—not on an individual basis. It is the very differences within the ensemble that give it power when joined together. No one thinks twice about building an ensemble with diverse skill sets, joining excellent writers with individuals who are stronger actors, and in turn pairing them with the most nimble improvisers. Is it such a leap, then, to think that building an ensemble that also considers socioeconomic background, age, sexuality, gender, or race might result in a group dynamic whose collective perspective might be capable of generating far more powerful and significant contributions to the culture at large than an ensemble where everyone is male, white, and straight?

If we hadn't actively chosen to be an inclusive organization some twenty-odd years ago, there's no telling how many stories would never have been told. We could not have been as effectively satiric when the nation elected our first black president had we not been blessed with actors of color in the ensembles. When immigration issues dominated the news, the fact that we had Latino actors on the stage allowed us to dissect that issue from a variety of angles. More recently, gay marriage has dominated the news cycle, and the LGBT members of our casts have created some remarkable pieces around that hot-button issue.

Without our diversity initiative, we might never have experienced the particular genius of a young mixed-race actor named Keegan-Michael Key in the seminal Second City e.t.c. revue, *Holy War, Batman*, or *The Yellow Cab of Courage*, developed in the wake of 9/11. The entire show revolved around a Pakistani cab driver, played by Key, driving through the streets of Chicago in the days immediately following the attack on the World Trade Center. Key's character encounters every manner of reaction to the event—xenophobes, apologists, the angry, and the sad. In an effort to avoid the violence that befell other Americans of Middle Eastern descent after the attacks, Keegan's character has draped his cab in American flags while blasting patriotic songs by Lee Greenwood, all in an effort to mask his ethnicity. Two new passengers, played by Andy Cobb and Sam Albert, get into his car.

ANDY Where are you from?
KEEGAN Me? I am from America.
ANDY No, like, where are you from, from?
KEEGAN Canada.

SAM   I think he means, like, where are you from originally?

KEEGAN   Well, it's a very long story, boss. You know, I
am from America via Canada, by way of (mumbling and
covering his mouth, barely audible) Pakistan.

ANDY   That's all right. We're all batting on the same
team.

KEEGAN   Yeah, but who wants to talk about Pakistan,
right? America! America! America!

SAM   Actually, I am a little bothered by the way everyone
is waving the flag around like some sort of Band-Aid for
the political wounds of this country.

KEEGAN   Ohhh! Narcolepsy. (Keegan slumps in his seat.
Andy wakes him up.) Oh, I am sorry. Every time someone
talks like that, I have a narcoleptic fit. We don't want to get
in a crash so . . . you better shut up.

That scene and that character would never have happened if
our ensemble hadn't included individuals whose entire lives could
speak to some deeper understanding of ostracism due to the color
of their skin.

Our organization has benefited greatly in seeking out new
and diverse voices to become part of our community. But building diversity requires more than hanging out a shingle that says
"Individuals of all races, genders, and sexual orientations are welcome." First of all, that sign is way too long. Second, you have to
implement a diversity initiative through a variety of approaches.

A diverse approach to hiring has provided us with countless
other opportunities. We are currently developing an improvisational course specifically geared toward seniors. We seed the
work in young people by doing outreach into schools and communities; we bring a variety of voices into our physical space

through workshops, lectures, and open houses; we build communities within our own community. A collection of Latino performers in our school and on our stages led to Loco, a bilingual troupe that explores comedy from a Latino perspective. This new group represents another part of the revolution: According to the Pew Research Center, nearly one in five Americans will be an immigrant in 2050; the Latino population will triple and will account for most of the nation's population growth for the next twenty-five years; whites will represent 47 percent of the population by 2050.[12]

The numbers are changing. But this is about more than numbers.

HELP YOUR TEAM BECOME AN ENSEMBLE NOW

We don't all have the luxury of building ensembles from scratch or of picking our fellow team members. More often than not, we are leading or are part of teams that have been thrown together by matters of convenience or entropy. So how do you create better ensembles with the people you are working with right now? And how can you as an individual help make greater contributions to your team? By following some classic principles straight from the improviser's handbook:

Be in the Moment
When we hire someone at The Second City, we focus on selecting people who know how to stay in the moment. It's the unifying character trait that made powerhouses out of Stephen Colbert, Tina Fey, Adam McKay, and countless other alumni that have graced the stages of The Second City. They all had

a steadfast ability to focus on the work right in front of them, whether they were rehearsing a thirty-second sketch from a 1977 Toronto revue or improvising onstage at the Kennedy Center in Washington, D.C., for hundreds of blue-haired society matrons who are actively disliking you and the comedy you are performing for them. True story. They really hated our 1995 show *Piñata Full of Bees*. It took a lot of effort for the ensemble to stay in the moment during that run.

While no one is ever capable of being in the moment twenty-four hours a day, seven days a week (unless you are ensconced in a Buddhist monastery—and odds are that the improv scene there is not that vibrant), it is essential that we recognize the moments in our workday when we must make our full selves fully present.

When you are in dialogue with your coworkers, stay present in the discussion at hand and don't dwell on previous mistakes or even previous successes. There is time for reflection and there is time for planning, both of which are distinct and separate from the time for creation and innovation. In short, if you are in a space where you are expected to bring your creative voice, it is vital that you stay in the moment. All your energies must be concentrated on the here and now so that your here and now is the best it can be and your fellow improvisers get to work with the best material you have to offer. If you are worrying about your next scene or your last scene; if your focus becomes about the audition for *Saturday Night Live*; if you get caught up in an internal critique of the dud of a line that you just improvised in front of 300 strangers—you will not succeed in this work.

In one-on-one meetings with colleagues, don't check e-mail and don't answer any calls. Focus on the person in front of you; listen to what they are saying as well as to what they are *not* saying. Creating a space where a fully engaged conversation can take place is part of staying in the moment. This will not only earn you the respect of your colleagues, it will also make it more likely that they will choose to engage and confide in you, giving you a decided edge in your organization.

In group meetings it can be even harder to stay present. Not every conversation will always be relevant to every attendee. But that makes it even more important that everyone involved stay engaged, especially if you hold higher status in the group. The minute one colleague sees you slipping off, it gives everyone permission to disengage and start building silos. Keep meetings short and focused. As Scott Adsit's intelligence-challenged company Vice President character said to a beleaguered HR director in the classic scene "Gump," "I'm a busy man, Jerry; I've got things to Vice."

Being in the moment is a philosophy that runs throughout our entire beginning-level classes at The Second City. It is part of the foundation for improvising. One of the exercises that can help train you to stay in the present is Mirror. You may already know how to do this, as it's a part of many training programs, theatrical and otherwise. Simply have the members of your group split up into pairs and face each other. Assign one person the job of initiating small movements with his face and body; the other person's job is to mirror his every action, gesture, or expression. Then have the pair reverse roles. Finally, see if they can continue to mirror each other when no one is assigned to lead.

Just as athletes stretch their limbs before they race, individuals who want to improve their emotional intelligence need to warm up those muscles as well. The Mirror exercise helps you practice focusing on others. It's a basic building block to being in an ensemble. Beginning students are prone to try to make their mirror exercise more interesting—by finding ways to make their scene partner laugh, for instance—but in this exercise, interesting doesn't matter. The goal is to achieve and sustain focus.

Give and Take

We're often asked what makes one show better or worse than another. Our shows at The Second City routinely sell out and our customer satisfaction reports are overwhelmingly excellent. But while we all have our favorites, there's almost universal agreement inside the whole building when a show just isn't that great, even though audiences are coming to the theatre in droves and laughing their way through the evening. When there is discontent in the ensemble, the show invariably isn't up to the standards of the brand. Most likely, the ensemble has failed to Give and Take in equal measure. There are, invariably, Givers and Takers, but the individuals in the ensemble need to do both in order to build with collective vigor.

Sheldon Patinkin, who has worked as a director and teacher at The Second City for more than fifty years, puts an interesting spin on the axiom "you're only as good as your weakest member." He offers that "at Second City, your ensemble is only as good as its ability to compensate for its weakest member." The difference is that, in our case, the onus for the weakness is put back on the ensemble rather than the individual. This strikes at the core of the concept of Give and Take.

For any scene to work, you need a balance of Givers and Takers. Sometimes people just don't like to share the spotlight, so they interrupt or otherwise block the Giver's attempts to take focus. Sometimes, people are just natural Takers. At The Second City, John Belushi, Bill Murray, and Chris Farley come to mind immediately. The minute any one of those performers stepped on the stage they took the focus, whether they wanted to or not. In an office setting, the same can occur for an individual who naturally dominates a conversation without even meaning to. But problems can also arise when Givers don't step up—when they don't jump in and take the focus when called upon to do so.

Recently, at a social media conference, we attended an interactive forum led by a young expert in the field. Minutes into the event, our "expert" was so bereft of focus that she reduced a group of attentive, responsible adults into chattering junior high school students. We spent the rest of the session wishing we could pull this person into an improv class simply to teach her how to take focus.

Do you practice Give and Take at your job? You should. Look at the successful entrepreneurs in your midst. How do they Give and Take? Management professor Adam Grant's research shows that people who practice Give and Take enjoy greater professional success than those who don't. Studying a variety of professional fields, Grant categorized the main players in the workforce as givers, matchers, and takers. He notes of a particular study, "The engineers with the highest productivity and the fewest mistakes were those who did far more favors for colleagues than they received. Engineers who took at least as much as they gave were more likely to have average results; the givers went to the extremes. The same pattern emerged in medicine and sales: The highest achievers were those most driven to help others."[13]

Give and Take doesn't have to be a solo endeavor. You can instill a Give and Take ethic throughout your organization. It requires that everyone on staff assume responsibility for the business. Successful business ensembles blend easily and respectfully across divisions. Give and Take makes us stay aware of others, ourselves, and the positive results we earn when working in a dynamic that knows that the whole is greater than the sum of its parts.

Give and Take behavior can include:

- Providing mentorship and counsel to any employee who may need it.

- Washing a few dirty dishes left in the break room, whether you left them or not.
- Attending special events celebrating individual or group celebrations, regardless of which area of the company that success happened in.
- Taking the time to try and learn everyone's name.

Give and Take is as simple as showing respect. Mastering Give and Take will not only provide a boon to your organization, it will also significantly boost your own role inside the ensemble. It may be surprising to some, but being a good ensemble member or a good teammate or a good colleague is an excellent way to spur personal growth.

As with all things, making Give and Take an organic part your interaction with others can take some practice. And as we pointed out, some people don't even realize that they lean too far in one direction or the other, whether excessively dominant or too unassertive. Because of this reality, just talking to employees about their ability to give and take focus is generally not enough. It's when they perform the exercise that they feel the distinction and behaviors can change.

Remember the Mirror exercise, which trained you to focus on someone else? The Give and Take exercise teaches you to pass that focus around the room.

The team spreads out in the room. Calling out individuals one by one, ask each person to practice giving focus to another team member using a simple physical cue, such as looking them in the eye, pointing at them, or touching them on the shoulder— any movement that puts the focus on the other person. Next, individuals are asked to take focus in the same manner. They can jump next to the person or block them from the rest of the room. Finally, you challenge the group to do both—give focus, then take focus, then give it back. Ideally, the various team members become adept at giving and taking focus in equal measure. Or it creates chaos in the room. Either result is a lesson. When it works seamlessly and ensemble members share focus, with some giving and some taking, they find a way to make order out of the exchange. When it doesn't work, everyone is confused and nothing gets accomplished.

Imagine you are at a business meeting where one person is constantly taking focus and if he does cede attention to someone else, it's only momentary and is quickly seized again. The other individuals in the meeting will disengage, either through anger or boredom. It makes collaboration impossible. A similar negative outcome happens if someone only gives focus—they don't add to the conversation, and they are forcing everyone else to do the work. In either case, mastering Give and Take makes for far more successful meetings.

If you can instill an ability among your coworkers to practice Give and Take in addition to Staying in the Moment, you are setting the foundation for increased and more productive communication.

Surrender the Need to Be Right

The need to be right, among individuals, institutions, and organizations, is one of the biggest barriers to an ensemble approach to creativity and innovation. Small actions can create big chasms.

The need to be right runs rampant in our lives. It was another theatre guy who coined the phrase "to err is human." And there is a reason that it is still part of the daily lexicon some 400 years after Shakespeare wrote it. We humans are imperfect. We make mistakes. Sometimes we're right, but sometimes we're wrong. This is a basic presupposition with which we imagine 99 percent of the world would agree. Which is why it is so stunning that so many people feel the need to be 100 percent right 100 percent of the time.

Take a moment and think about the most difficult people you have encountered, be it in your office, in your family, as part of an organization, or at an event.

What made these people so awful to deal with? Did they have an agenda? Did they have a "my way or the highway" attitude? Did they listen to anyone's voice but their own? Chances are, they had an insatiable need to be right and would rather piss off everyone else than surrender an inch. These people are destructive; they keep innovation at bay.

If you can create an ensemble where everyone agrees to surrender the need to be right, you will increase productivity by leaps and bounds. You will create an environment where innovation can flourish; you will also make everyone happier.

Make no mistake; the power of the need to be right is not easily broken. And unfortunately, it's most prevalent in individuals who have just enough power to make life miserable for everyone around them. If you are in a position to engage the person in your company who always needs to be right, find a way—any way—to get them to agree to try taking a Yes, And approach to their work for a day. You might remember the Yes, And exercise from Chapter Two: Participants have to eliminate the word *no* from their vocabulary. For one day, they have to say "yes" and they have to say "and" in response to whatever is said to them or in whatever situation they find themselves.

Then, sit back and watch that person explode with frustration and anger: You have just taken away their automatic response to any point of view that might challenge their own. You have forced them to speak using the verbal cues of inclusion, partnership, and respect. And it's killing them.

We saw this happen when a major cultural institution in Chicago asked us to lead a workshop in teamwork. We gave them an overview on the kinds of workshops that we lead, but first, we asked to meet with them to talk about the specifics of how the team was currently operating and what they hoped to gain from the workshop. Fifteen minutes into our debrief, the client came clean. The entire reason for considering the workshop was a single employee—someone at a senior level with valuable skills—who was making everyone else's daily life a living hell. Let's call him Jim. Jim didn't listen to others' ideas; he belittled coworkers both under and over him; his arrogance on every subject had become a morale killer for every staffer who had to work with him. But Jim was also an expert in his field, and the group wanted to try to make it work.

The instructor started by doing what we call status exercises. People jockey for status all the time, in every aspect of their lives. Since art imitates reality, it is important for anyone in comedy to understand status—what it means to have it, lose it, even never have it at all. The instructor put Jim in a grouping with members of the staff who worked under him. She told him that, for the purposes of this exercise, he had to maintain low status during their conversation. Jim could speak only if spoken to, he needed to be physically lower than others in the room, and he needed to support everyone's ideas but his own.

Jim didn't enjoy this.

The instructor asked the group for a topic of conversation around the office that was prone to create conflict. Everyone agreed that whenever they tried to talk about making their very old institution more modern, things tended to get heated. This time, Jim, who was sometimes affectionately referred to as old school, was told he had to hold his tongue during the conversation. As others offered all kinds of ideas—some quite bold—Jim squirmed in his seat. He began to turn red and then suddenly burst to his feet and literally stopped the exercise.

In front of a number of witnesses, Jim had to confront the fact that he had an almost insatiable need to be the one voice in the room that was always louder than the rest. It was almost impossible for him even to pretend to be an equal member of the team. We coached Jim to think of himself as an actor in a scene his group was performing to help him digest what he was hearing without judging it or getting emotional. Jim didn't speak thereafter, but it was clear that he wasn't really listening, as the instructor tried to appeal to his intellect and implore him to consider an alternative way to behave in the group dynamic.

Jim was given the Yes, And assignment for the next day. By all reports, it was a miserable failure.

But here's the deal—we know we can't eliminate Jims from our working environment and we're not trying to. In fact, having a Jim in the room can be absolutely crucial. Sometimes a group needs a leader willing to speak up and make an unpopular decision; sometimes expertise and knowledge really do mean one person's opinions carry more weight than others. At The Second City, directors are constantly making decisions about what material gets cut and what stays in during the final weeks before a show opens. That's a director's prerogative; directors have earned that right by virtue of the job title and the expertise that got them there. But leaders can make big decisions without being bullies—that is, without being Jims.

Individuals with authority get to make big decisions. They also get to act with inclusion, charity, and respect. None of those qualities need detract from or diminish their status as a decision maker. In an atmosphere dominated by those who will never surrender the need to be right, every disappointment is magnified, and decisions are met with recrimination and even outright hostility. Exclusionary, reproachful, and unkind leadership is not only a morale killer, it is also likely to reduce the productivity of the individuals suffering under it.

There is a place for Jim within a company dynamic, but only in isolation and only for a limited time; the long-term wear and tear of a Jim is just too great.

Jim didn't take to our improv approach. Jim got canned.

Bullies don't usually know they're bullies. The good news is that bullying can be unlearned. We saw this happen recently in a very surprising way.

Like many companies, The Second City will distribute an RFP (request for proposal) when we are looking to hire an outside company to help us build a new system or consult on a major project. In the process, we meet with a lot of business teams whose job it is to land us as their client. When we recently sent out an RFP for help with a digital initiative, we were fortunate to meet with some of the most cutting-edge tech firms in the business. One company, based in New York, took the time to visit us on multiple occasions. The owner of the company, Devin, took a personal interest in landing us as a client. He not only led every discussion we had, he also immersed himself in the culture of The Second City—seeing all the shows, taking classes, reading up on all the literature about us and our field. We were impressed by his attention; he was an impressive guy: Ivy League schooling; two successful start-up companies that he sold for a lot of money; and a fairly significant amount of good press in various industry journals. Perfect candidate, perfect approach. So what went wrong? After our third meeting with Devin, the senior management team stayed in the boardroom to recap the conversation. One of the newest executives on our team queried the room, "Is anyone else feeling relentlessly bulldozed in these conversations?" That one question opened the floodgates; every single member of our management team who had been in both one-on-one and one-and-group conversations with Devin nodded their heads and quickly started citing examples: he interrupted others when they talked; if he wasn't the focus of the conversation, he would check e-mails on his smartphone; he almost never allowed a member of his own team to speak, and if they did, he was likely to contradict them. It wasn't that he wasn't a pleasant or smart guy—he had an affable personality—he just couldn't resist the sound of his own voice. His attitude actually became a deal breaker: We needed to work with a team and there wasn't a team there. There was a guy— and that guy was going to drive us crazy.

In business, people almost never tell you the real reasons you didn't get the job. In this case, the newest member of our team did something kind of great. He told Devin exactly why he didn't get the business. Cut to six months later, and we get a call from Devin. He's in town and wants to take a few of us to lunch. Pleasantries are exchanged and Devin says the following: "I wanted to tell you how appreciative I am for your honesty about the reasons that you didn't go with our company. Frankly, it was the most distraught I've [ever] been about not getting a new client. I love your work and I really got invested in the culture of your company. I continued taking improv classes in New York, and this whole experience taught me that I wasn't the right leader for our company. So I demoted myself." Devin did what very few successful leaders do: He allowed himself to look in the mirror, recognize that change was needed, and he changed. He brought in a leadership consultant who agreed with both our and Devin's personal assessment of his leadership. They crafted a plan: Devin would get training on being more collaborative and communicative; he would promote his general manager to company president; and the company would undergo a cultural transformation that would protect itself from any one voice that sought to drown out the others.

There is no special water that you drink at The Second City to kill off the need to be right, but we honestly don't see a lot of that kind of behavior. In the course of improvising with an ensemble, you quickly learn that nothing works if you cling to your idea of what's right, true, or funny. Improvisation demands that you surrender to the greater needs of the ensemble.

To be honest, the axiom "surrender the need to be right" sounds more likely to be found in Buddhism, but it is also inherent in improvisation. It's all about recognizing that you are only a part of a greater whole, and that in letting go and ceding control you open yourself up to possibilities you may never have imagined. Many of the exercises we share here, such as Gibberish Games and One-Word Story, are meant to reinforce this core principle. To build off the Give and Take exercise, we recommend another, called Parts of a Whole.

It works like this: The instructor gets the team on their feet and gives them a suggestion, such as the name of an animal. The team members must silently organize themselves into the shape of that animal by molding themselves into body parts, or otherwise inserting themselves into the picture (by pretending to be a pond or a tree, for example). The next suggestion could be, people in a restaurant. One by one, individuals adopt the positions needed to create that tableau. If two people are seated facing each other, a team member will move to stand over them like a waiter, while another may pose as though he were pouring water, as a busboy might.

The exercise reinforces why it's so critical to be able to cede control and learn to play a part that contributes to the greater whole. Here is how Second City alum and famed improvisational teacher Avery Schreiber explained the importance of this tenet:

"It's the magic that happens when two people surrender their need to control, and create something that neither would have made on their own."

Practicing improv strengthens the muscles that allow us to stay in the moment, give and take, and sacrifice that part of us that thinks being right actually matters. In turn, those muscles allow us to become better improvisers—and innovators.

THE CO-CREATION
STORY, OR AUDIENCES
WANT IN ON THE ACT

For our 1998 revue, *The Psychopath Not Taken*, the ensemble developed a scene that began with a robbery at a vault containing "all the gold in Metropolis." But before the bank robbers make their escape, Superman enters the scene. Except in this version, the superhero, in flowing red cape, rolls onto the stage in a wheelchair.

That moment elicited a response from the audience that ranged from disappointed groan to outright indignant hostility. Just a couple of years earlier, famed film actor Christopher Reeve, best known for his dashing portrayal of Superman, had been paralyzed in a horse-riding accident and permanently confined to a wheelchair.

We introduced this scene during the preview period, before a new show opens officially to the press and public, during which the ensemble and director tinker with material to make sure it's working to maximum effect. In this case, the audience made clear that the material had gone too far. One preview night, alum Martin Short was in the audience. The moment actor Rich Talarico rolled onto the stage as Superman, Martin couldn't help himself and howled, "Nooooooo!"

At The Second City, we create our shows in constant dialogue with our audience. This doesn't mean we cater to the specific comic tastes of each person who walks into the theatre, nor does it mean that we use them like focus groups, only keeping the material that generates the greatest amount of applause. What it means is that we listen to their reactions—their laughter, for sure, but also their groans and even their silences. In response, we edit, change, and hone our content to make the material as strong as possible. We don't surrender our own expertise in the craft of making comedy, but we do invite the audience into our process. They give us information every single evening, thus becoming an essential ingredient in the creative process.

In the case of the Superman scene, it was up to the ensemble and the director, Mick Napier, to decide if the scene was worth trying to salvage in a new form. Mick wanted to keep the scene, but he didn't want to alienate the audience. So he went home one night and wrote a song for the Superman character to sing—an anthem that would break the fourth wall of the production, allowing the audience to see that we, too, were aware of how shocking the image was, but that would also make a satiric point about celebrity, hero worship, and the often bizarre line between fiction and reality. During the next preview performance, in the midst of foiling the bank robbery, Superman rose from his wheelchair and sang:

> *And I'll cherish each moment.*
> *Each second that passes again.*
> *What I'd give for the choice to sit down or a smile that's not*
>   *fighting a frown.*

Or a chance to rewrite that strange day when I fell to the ground.

The audience was still aghast that Superman had rolled onto the stage in a wheelchair, but by the time he finished the song, the audience was back on our side. The scene stayed in the show and became one of the most talked-about pieces of that era.

The Superman scene was transformed from a heartless, tactless exploitation of someone's misfortune into a sharp, funny, yet poignant commentary on the random injustice and irony of life through a process called co-creation. Whether you're developing comedy, marketing slogans, better paths to production, or efficiency on the factory floor, co-creation provides remarkable insight and helps ensure that while breaking new ground or creating new products, you're always giving your customers what they want, even if they are unable to tell you it's what they want.

In this chapter, we will look at how The Second City co-creates with its audience and how businesses can apply those same models and processes to improve their own communication loop with their customers. Beyond customer applications, we will examine how co-creation can thrive among your own internal ensembles, and we'll share a few case studies of companies that have successfully used improvisation as a method by which to measure their own brand essence and customer loyalty. We'll also give you some practical exercises to apply when co-creating both internally and externally.

IMPROVE CO-CREATION IN-HOUSE

There are three keys to co-creating successfully within your own business and ensemble:

1. Find *the* Idea, Not *Your* Idea

While individuals can come up with great ideas, ensembles that are willing to co-create are ultimately better and more consistent at finding *the* idea. This concept can be a hard sell, because when an ensemble is engaged in co-creation, ideas no longer belong to the individual who came up with them. Rather, they belong to the group. We are generally programmed to run with our own ideas so we can control the idea's outcome and enjoy the credit; we are not inclined to allow other people to augment or change our ideas, especially when they are good. So if you want to co-create to get to *the* idea, you first have to encourage people to cede control over their ideas for the greater good of the group.

2. Cede Control

Getting people to cede control often becomes exponentially more difficult the higher you rise up the food chain. Chances are, the top creative thinkers in your organization are not inclined to share. This is unfortunate since, in our experience, creatives willing to cede control over ideas gain a more robust fount of insights than individuals who prefer to go it alone. Our best creatives at The Second City boast an unflinching ability to generate ideas, along with a deft aptitude for closing their mouths and listening to all the ensemble members, thus allowing an idea to gestate, change, and morph from a single morsel into a rich, complex, and tasty dish.

The development of The Second City's televised sketch comedy show, *SCTV*, our answer to *Saturday Night Live*, provides an excellent example of how co-creation can generate tremendous creative energy, and how that energy can be quashed when someone—usually an executive—tries to control it. Starting in 1976, when the show was a low-budget production based in

Canada, the cast was free to create their characters and material in the classic Second City improvisational style. The results were incredibly rich: Johnny LaRue, The Schmenge Brothers, Count Floyd, Ed Grimley—the list of memorable characters goes on and on. Some of them were co-created when the actors joined forces with hair, makeup, and wardrobe personnel, a potent resource that writers and performers often neglect. Others were born out of Improv Sets developed through collaborations between writers with Second City credentials and writers from other comic backgrounds. The success of the whole show was grounded in its phenomenally co-creative, no-holds-barred mix.

But when the show was picked up by NBC in 1981, the network began trying to bring in new show runners to "lead" the show—talented individuals who were used to the more traditional creative model of "you create what I tell you to create." One after another came and went, frustrated by their failure to inflict their creative will upon an ensemble who knew how it worked best. Up until then, the improvisational model that this cast had followed in collaboration with its producing partners had worked wonderfully. But that creative ecosystem was hindered, not helped, by network officials and more traditional television executives whose comfort zone was strictly hierarchical.

SCTV would go on to be nominated for fifteen Emmy Awards, launching the careers of stars like John Candy, Martin Short, Eugene Levy, Catherine O'Hara, Rick Moranis, and many others, and earn recognition as one of the greatest sketch comedy shows of all time. But eventually it became clear that the network would always need to be the loudest voice in the room. The fatigue from constantly fighting to defend a creative process that was proven to work took its toll. Cast members started leaving the show, and *SCTV* ended its run in 1984.

3. Eradicate Fear

There are several main blockades to good co-creation. In our experience, every one of them stems from fear.

- Fear of failure
- Fear of looking foolish
- Fear of the unknown

Fear may be a useful emotion for keeping us safe, ensuring that we floss, or making sure we turn in our taxes, but it's detrimental to the act of group creativity. Fear does not inspire elegant creative thinking; it inspires knee-jerk, path-of-least-resistance ideas. When used as a motivational tool, fear may push someone to run harder, but it's never going to push anyone to run smarter. No organization or business will ever gain creative advantage when governed by fear.

Fear allowed myriad employees and executives at Enron to stay silent when they knew company executives were awash in illegal business practices that would doom the entire organization. Fear of killing off their film business eventually killed Kodak. (Ironically, it was a Kodak employee who invented the first digital camera, in 1975.) Fear of losing season ticket buyers kept the Chicago Blackhawks off of television for decades, ensuring years of a declining audience base and brand erosion until ownership passed to Rocky Wirtz, who reversed his dad's decision and put the Hawks back on TV in 2008. Two years later the stadium was packed for every game and the team even went on to win the Stanley Cup.

Nothing could be worse for co-creation than a scaredy-cat culture. It's almost impossible to live and create in a moment when you're wracked by fear. We know this because we've seen plenty of examples of fear-induced mistakes and missteps over

the course of casting and running our theatre for so long, especially during auditions.

Every year, hundreds of young improvisers come onstage for
fifteen minutes or so to work in front of producers, directors, and
teachers, trying to get one of the coveted few spots in The Second
City system. It is, without doubt, the most anxiety-riddled event
that occurs at the theatre. For so many of the young people who
audition each year, this job is a life's dream. The pressure is
intense as these young hopefuls warm up in the theatre lobby
before they take the stage, and the stakes get only higher when
the stage doors open. The best improvisers find a way to put
their fears aside. They improvise freely and loosely; they make
smart and defined choices; they take care of their scene partners
and they let their unique sense of humor shine through in all the
choices they make onstage. That's about 10 percent of the people
we see over a full week of auditions, and they are usually the ones
who get a job with us.

The other 90 percent offer us a fascinating display of the multitude of ways in which humans externalize their fear. Over time,
we've noticed a few manifestations that are particularly destructive to performers and that manage to subvert the ability of a
group to create anything of substance or humor. You may recognize them, too; people use these same tactics all the time in every
organization when they are trying to hide their fear.

Asking Questions

We don't mean to suggest that you shouldn't be inquisitive or,
worse, assume you have all the answers. But one of the very early
rules you learn in studying improv is to avoid asking questions of
your scene partner. When improvising a scene, you're supposed
to be in dialogue, creating together. When you ask questions,
however, you put the onus on your partner, and your partner

alone, to provide the content and laughs for the material you are supposed to be creating together. People improvising in fear ask questions because they are too afraid—too inside their own heads—to put themselves on the line and take responsibility for making the kinds of declarative offerings that serve to build the content of a scene.

Here's how it might play out onstage:

GOOD IMPROVISER I love this time of year in Chicago. It makes you forget how terrible it is the other nine months.

A great initiation. The good improviser has placed the scene in a time and place—it's summer in Chicago.

FEAR IMPROVISER Why are we here?

The question provides no information for the scene partner to build upon. It basically pushes the creative act back upon the Good Improviser.

GOOD IMPROVISER You know why we're here. We're here to get great tans, meet people, and maybe save some folks from drowning.

OK, the Good Improviser has us back on track. Without seeking to lessen the status of the scene partner, this information affirms that everyone onstage is in this together, knowingly. And now it's clear that the pair are lifeguards.

FEAR IMPROVISER But what if I can't swim?

This scene is going nowhere. The Fear Improviser is blocking every new piece of information and throwing it back at Good Improviser. The problem is not that Fear Improviser has introduced a lifeguard that can't swim (that could actually be pretty funny). The problem is the way he has introduced it. He's blocking, not building, the scene. He's throwing curve balls and challenging Good Improviser to figure out how to handle them. It's not fair to Good Improviser, it's not funny, and the customers want their money back.

How might the same sort of scenario play out in a business setting, say at a brainstorm for the marketing of a new product?

> **GOOD MARKETER**   OK, everybody, our client has introduced a new craft beer. It's aimed at men ages twenty-five to thirty-five, living in urban markets, and with disposable income.

A clear initiative to start the brainstorm—naming the product and its audience.

> **FEAR MARKETER**   Well, who would actually buy that beer?

Good Marketer has already established the audience for the beer. With this question, Fear Marketer undermines the validity of the information already put on the table.

> **GOOD MARKETER**   The demographic is pretty specific: young men who live in the city. But you're right, we don't need to pigeonhole our creative ideas to sell the product this early in the brainstorm. Any idea is a good idea at this point.

The Good Marketer has restored order to the meeting without challenging the negativity of the Fear Marketer, and the room has been reopened to all ideas.

FEAR MARKETER Really? I only want to hear great ideas.

And all paths to open and honest creativity are shut down. Fear Marketer is usually using questions to hide his fear of not being creative enough and being unable to provide *the* idea.

There is a place and time for asking questions. You need to know details in order to contribute to the greater conversation. But once those details have been shared, it's time for the team to get creative and brainstorm. At that point, questions are a creativity killer.

Aggression

We often see novice improvisers choose to hide behind aggression. When you think about it, it's not surprising. Sigmund Freud wrote, "The tendency of aggression is an innate, independent, instinctual disposition in man . . . it constitutes the most powerful obstacle to culture."[14] In other words, when we're afraid, we lash out. It happens in real life and, guess what, it happens onstage.

In the mid-'90s, an actor who had clearly lied about his improvisational training on his résumé came in with his fellow actors, all of whom had taken years of classes in the art form. It's a testament as to how overtly audacious and aggressive his improvisational choices were that day that many of us still remember his name and could pick him out of a crowd, even though we spent only fifteen minutes with him nearly twenty years ago. We'll call him Ray for the purposes of this story. Ray's first improvisational choice was to kill his scene partner before any words were spoken.

Scene over. His second choice was to scream his dialogue without ever allowing his fellow scene partner the opportunity to speak a single word. At that point, the incredibly patient director leading the auditions suggested to the whole group that they give each other space to talk, that they lower their voices, and that they choose to improvise scenes wherein no one was fighting or arguing. He said it to the group, but he was really saying it to Ray.

The next time Ray initiated a scene—and it's burned into our collective memory forever—he screamed, "I'm a zit on Bill Clinton's ass!" To be fair, he did stop there and left space for his fellow improviser to speak. We believe the poor fellow actor sharing the stage with him responded gamely with, "I think we are all perplexed by this situation." (Don't worry; we let the other actors onstage re-audition with more experienced players.)

Weeks later we received a three-page letter from Ray, asking us why he wasn't hired on the spot. "I was the guy who was the zit on Bill Clinton's ass!" he wrote. "And everything just stopped. It was amazing!"

He was right. It was amazing how everything just stopped. The problem is, that's the last thing you want to see happen during the creative process, onstage or off. There is no question that dealing with aggressive personalities is very difficult. If you're a boss, the answer is simple: Dictate the code of behavior that you expect from all your team members—a code that mandates sharing the stage and co-creating with respect. Then give those personalities practice to improve. They will need to unlearn what's become second nature to them.

If you're not the boss, well, that's tougher. Can HR help? Can you enlist other leaders in your organization who agree that such behavior is damaging to a culture? If not, you might follow the advice we offered an audience member at a panel discussion at Chicago Ideas Week, who said, "Your ideas seem great in theory, but my boss—the only person I can report to—does all the horrible things you're talking about. So what do I do?" It took a couple of seconds before we both said, "Quit."

Yelling

Another way people manifest their fear and prevent co-creation is simply to make themselves louder than anyone else in the room, or bulldoze their way through interactions until people just do what they want them to do. We've all seen plenty of these examples of leadership by brute force. In fact, it's often rewarded in the workplace. That doesn't make it right.

Studies recently published in the *Journal of Applied Psychology* highlight the problems that arise in aggressive work environments where yelling is commonplace. Researchers found that a boss's verbal aggression hurts employees' memories, making it difficult for them to understand instructions. In addition, individuals who handled complaints from hostile, aggressive customers had more difficulty remembering the nature of the complaint lobbed at them than employees who spoke with calm customers.[15]

The collateral damage of management-by-volume is significant and long lasting. Any sense of collaboration is thrown out the window; a culture of "me" permeates the business rather than a culture of "we," and morale is terrible. It's almost impossible to co-create and build for the future in this kind of environment.

If you deal with someone like this, you need to understand the impetus for the behavior before you have a fighting chance to address the root problem. People who yell, and bullies in general, are acting out of fear and insecurity. The only way to change their behavior is to help them feel safe and secure. Fortunately, improvisers have the tools at hand to achieve such a goal, for many of the elements of improv like Yes, And, Give and Take, and listening are conducive to this kind of effort.

Waffling

Yet another symptom of fear is to freeze and avoid doing anything resembling taking a position, making a declarative statement, or giving an opinion. Instead, fearful people waffle:

"I don't know."

"It could be, but I'm not sure."

"If you say so."

"Maybe."

Waffling is such a predominant activity of the fearful improviser that it's become a penalty in a variety of improvisational games. Waffling is merely a delaying tactic, something you do when you are too afraid to leap into the unknown. Unfortunately, waffling is an all-too-common refuge for people put in the position to make decisions, but who lack the confidence to act. In business, not making a decision is almost worse than making the wrong decision. The secret to building confidence is practice.

Improvisers warm up to prepare before going onstage. They do vocal exercises, they stretch, and they psych themselves up with their fellow ensemble members by looking them in the eye while exchanging visual and verbal cues. They will gather in a circle and pretend they are throwing a ball around. When improvisers are in practice, it means they have made sure they have rehearsed enough times to know their material cold before taking the stage in front of an audience. Good performers take all their preparation and practice and put it to work, leaving their fear aside and allowing themselves to act in the moment. To successfully co-create, they know they first have to be *ready* to co-create.

It's no different in the workplace. You know you are prepared for your big meeting or your important interview when you have enough facts and data that allow you to fully understand the business issues at hand. But once you have that data, you can practice by creating scenarios with your fellow team members to test out ideas and get a feel for decisive leadership. You want to give yourself as many opportunities as possible to make decisions in real time and learn to ignore any voices of doubt or insecurity. If you can apply and embody the qualities of an improviser, you will be able to control your fear, and maybe even forget it as you listen, respond, co-create, and perform in the moment.

IMPROVE CO-CREATION WITH YOUR AUDIENCE

We've discussed why you must use all the principles of improvisation, such as listening, Yes, And, and Give and Take, to help you communicate better with your colleagues and form a true ensemble capable of creative breakthroughs and innovation. But co-creation isn't just something that should be reserved for in-house. At The Second City, we go even further by initiating and maintaining a real-time dialogue with our customers every time we perform. We solicit their opinions even as we're developing our material, so our audience—our consumer—is involved in our creative process from the get-go, particularly when we are creating new content during the rehearsal period of a new show. We come to the audience for topic suggestions; we gauge their real-time response to the material as it's being improvised and use it to inform further refinements of the material. Finally, we hone the finished product in direct dialogue with each audience leading up to the opening night.

We're not the only business in steady dialogue with its customers—we were just one of the first. We were interactive before start-ups and digital entrepreneurs made it a household word. Over the past decade, however, other organizations have followed suit, as they see the advantage enjoyed by organizations that welcome customer engagement. It's why companies maintain Facebook pages and monitor Twitter feeds. It's the reason for focus groups, silent shoppers, and SurveyMonkey.

Because co-creation requires promoting dialogues over monologues, at The Second City we often refer to it as Being in Dialogue. Outside the theatre, in innovation and new product development circles, you may have heard it referred to as real-time customer feedback, rapid prototyping, or crowdsourcing.

COMPUTER + CROWDSOURCING = COMEDY (SORT OF?)

In the early '90s, Stephen Colbert, ever the forward-looking satirist, decided to channel the amazing power of the World Wide Web for our Improv Set. One night, Colbert rounded up a handful of extension cords and brought one of the few computers in the building to the backstage area. Connecting all the extension cords, he placed the computer on a rolling cart and wheeled it onto the stage, where he announced to the audience that tonight we would also be soliciting audience interaction from the entire world via the Internet. The significant lack of audience reaction to this announcement should have been our first clue that history was not to be made on The Second City stage that night.

To get the full picture, imagine a twentysomething Stephen Colbert—hair a bit puffier, clothes far less tailored and pressed—obscured by a giant computer on a rickety coffee cart as his fellow ensemble members loiter around him onstage. The whir of the dial-up connection droned on for nearly a minute until Stephen was online and navigating his way to a preselected chat room where he intended to seek inspired suggestions from users for the cast to improvise on. He typed in, "We are live at The Second City. Give us a suggestion, and we will improvise a scene based on it." Then, Stephen, the cast, and the audience waited in awkward silence. No one responded. Finally, after nearly ten minutes, a kid from Indiana typed back one word: "Dildo."

So that didn't work. It wasn't the word itself that posed a problem. A master improviser like Colbert could probably build something funny around almost anything. The problem was the timing. The lengthy pause between Colbert's request and the response he finally got killed the scene's energy and momentum. Timing matters when it comes to co-creation, whether in improv or in business. In our world, even seconds between an audience member's suggestion and the response of an improviser can prove fatal to the success of what follows. And in business today, consumers expect a rapid response when they post a comment about a business or brand on social media. That's been hard for a lot of businesses to get used to. Of course, every business has to manage its own response time to customer inquiries, complaints, and suggestions. Yet while there is absolute value in a considered response that may take hours or even days, there is a different kind of value in an instantaneous reply. It may be a bit more challenging than taking your time, but the energy and fast, creative thinking a quick response requires can compel you to perform even better.

When you receive real-time customer feedback of the kind a live audience provides, there is no time to separate the generation of content from the analysis of content. As you improvise a scene onstage, you feel the effect of your work upon your audience immediately. Their reaction then affects the choices you make in real time. Because improvisation demands that you stay in the moment, you do it without worrying about the value or validity of your work, which frees you to be more spontaneous, creative, and authentic. Reserve your analysis for later when you review the tape or take notes from your director. In the moment of artistic inspiration, improvisers use real-time customer feedback as a co-creation tool. And so do many companies, especially those who employ social media to get closer to their customers.

CLOROX® LAUGHS THROUGH ICK WITH PARENTS ON TWITTER

As we write this book, we've just completed a very interesting and highly successful assignment with Clorox, in which we engaged Clorox consumers in a live, improvised award show on Twitter. Why would we do such a thing? Simple. To give Clorox a chance to show how laughable life's messes can be when you look beyond the mess, and to give parents a chance to share war stories about the ickier moments they encounter on a daily basis.

It turns out that Clorox products are really great at cleaning up the messes that we all make in our lives. Unseemly bathroom messes, embarrassing kitchen messes, toddler messes, messes people make when they're sick . . . you get the idea. And historically, people don't really talk about that stuff openly, and companies like Clorox didn't, either. But Clorox was seeing a new trend, with the modern moms and dads who represent a key target audience for their products. They are using social media to share stories and compare notes about the experiences and mishaps they encounter as parents, on many topics, which can be full of potential for comedy gold.

To make all this sharing possible, Clorox, public relations agency Ketchum, and influential dad bloggers from How To Be A Dad worked with us to create the Clorox Ick Awards, where we celebrated the ickier moments of everyday life. The Clorox Ick Awards show was hosted by famed Second City alum Rachel Dratch, who teamed up with an ensemble of Second City actors to enact scenes and funny monologues based on the real-life messes that parents shared with us on Twitter using #Ickies. Clorox shared the sketches in real-time with the Twitter audience for reaction and voting, before announcing the #Ickies winners in categories like #HorrificMess and #EpicMess.

Apparently, we tapped into something important in the parenting zeitgeist. During the four hours of the live awards show, #Ickies became a trending topic on Twitter and Clorox saw over *160 million* social media impressions from more than 16,800 tweets!

There are a couple key lessons in this. First, the funniest stuff is always grounded in truth, as evidenced by the crazy stories that real parents tweeted to us. And second, audiences will really respond when you let them in on the act. In the case of the Clorox Ick Awards, we wouldn't have had a show or event without actual parents, and the stunning success we saw was based entirely on our willingness to co-create a funny, novel, authentic, and occasionally messy event in the moment with our audience. Social media has created all sorts of new opportunities for companies to co-create with the people who buy their products, and as time goes by, more and more companies are thinking of inventive ways to let audiences in on the act.

Rapid Prototyping

We've had success using improv as part of a rapid prototyping process in product development as well. Recently, we were approached by an important research organization whose client, a major credit card company, was looking to gather new insights about their small-business-owner segment, so they could develop product improvements that would help them win more share of this demographic. We worked with them and their ad agency partners to get briefed on the market situation and ultimately recommended one of our improv ideation sessions, in which we do structured improv around key themes and ideas that are especially germane to small business owners. We did scenes about the pressures that come from poor cash management and bad receivables. We did scenes about the all-in lives of small business owners and the difficulty they have in separating their professional and personal lives. And, to really ground the session in reality, our client invited a group of small business owners to be part of our audience, to give us suggestions for our scenes and reactions to what rang true. There's nothing quite like shared laughter to bring people and organizations together. Following the improv sessions, the credit card company and the small business owners had a chance to talk. Their conversation revealed a number of painful areas, and their shared experience made it easier to discuss them candidly and productively. No one felt attacked or on the spot, because the hard truths had already been put at their feet and ridiculed by our performers.

In this context and others, the improv comedy process reveals new insights about customers and their challenges; it also encourages clients to tinker with messages and marketing ideas in real time, in front of their customers. This leads to a much more open exchange than the kind you'd see in typical research and focus group settings, and creates a forum in which client and customer actually co-create new product offerings, upending the traditional product development process.

Agencies in the advertising, PR, and design worlds are increasingly moving toward a model that favors ongoing co-creation with clients versus grand reveals of fully formed creative campaigns. Historically, agencies felt that the best way to demonstrate their expertise was to conceive a creative strategy and then sell clients on recommendations that had been developed with minimal client input. Conventional wisdom was that clients wouldn't value the agencies' output as much if they were allowed in on the development process. So agency creatives would squirrel themselves away, sometimes for weeks and months, before doing a high-stakes, "hope we got it right" presentation to their client counterparts.

The unintended consequence of this approach was to create a No, But dynamic instead of one more collaborative and Yes, And. Nobody likes to be sold an idea; they'd rather help create it, or at least have some chance to weigh in on it before being forced to make a final decision.

The move toward more co-creation is partly driven by the need for speed in business today. In a Don Draper world, you had time for martinis, chasing the client's wife, and a protracted and isolated creative development schedule. In today's climate, there's less time for on-the-job vices (we're told) and a sequestered creative process. Whatever is driving the move to co-creation, it is being welcomed by clients and agencies alike, who see new benefits in partnering to get to better ideas.

BUILT TO CO-CREATE

For the most part, if something works in our company, we don't bother to deconstruct it to figure out why it's working. For example, we've long known that co-creation with our audience works, but we've only recently learned why. It's the closure principle in action, or at least a variation on it. What is that, you ask? The closure principle stems from the world of neuroscience. At its essence, it states that when we view fragments of images that together form a nearly complete picture, we still "see" the missing information because our brains are wired to automatically fill in the gaps and missing pieces needed to complete the picture.

By now you certainly know that we're not brain scientists, but we find this intriguing idea relevant to our work because it shows that human beings are hardwired to contribute to incomplete ideas to make them whole, and they tend to respond positively when invited to contribute to an idea that isn't yet fully formed. Paradoxically, the closure principle is a door opener in our work. It's a core part of improv, driving co-creation and, science suggests, maybe even human nature.

IMPROV SETS—MAKING THE WORLD SAFE FOR CO-CREATION

As we've discussed, The Second City improvises to develop most of its performance material, but one of the crucial ingredients in our formula is something we've talked about a lot already, the third act of our show, the Improv Set.

The Improv Set is the research and development arm of our company. It's invaluable. Here's how it works:

Six actors, a musical director, a stage manager, and a director spend ten to twelve weeks creating a new Second City revue.

During the day, the actors rehearse new ideas, many of which are developed through improvisation, and some of which are brought in as scripted first drafts. This material is then tried out in front of the audience as part of the third act of the evening: the Improv Set.

The Improv Set is free, and this is key, because it lowers the stakes for everyone involved in the experience. Anyone walking by the theatre can pop in, free of charge (as long as there is an empty chair), to catch this final set of the evening. And because these improvised sets occur late at night, almost half of the paying audience gets up and leaves before the set begins, only to be replaced by a horde of twentysomethings who have queued up outside the theatre to see some free comedy. By presenting the set free of charge, we signal to the audience that they may get exactly what they paid for—bubkes. Of course, they might get lucky and witness a stroke of sheer brilliance. There's no way to know. But the audience can't complain if they don't like what they see because they entered the theatre at their own risk. This arrangement provides our actors, too, with a degree of safety, because it lessens the pressure to please anyone.

We send out other clues to our audience to help set the context for this distinct part of the three-act show. At the end of the two-act revue, the actors take their bows—a physical cue that a portion of the evening's entertainment has concluded. After the bows and applause, an actor reemerges onstage to do an "outro" (as opposed to an intro) wherein the audience is encouraged to overtip the waitstaff while the actor plugs other shows in the building. Finally the actor will ask, "Do you want to see a little more?" and explain that in ten minutes the cast will come back to perform a fully improvised third act, free of charge. All these physical and verbal cues provide the audience with the context they need to watch the upcoming improvised set with a new perspective.

Companies, too, benefit when they can engage with their audiences and solicit ideas. But engaging in full-blown co-creation on social media platforms such as Facebook and Twitter can be dangerous. They provide a certain level of free exchange with customers, but increasingly these tend to be high-risk, unfiltered exchanges. So some organizations have started conducting their own versions of Improv Sets. They still co-create with the public, but they do it on their own terms by establishing context and setting expectations, thereby creating safe, low-cost, low-risk, potentially high-return opportunities to connect with their customers, develop new products, new talent, and new lines of inquiry.

For example, in 2009, *Chicago Tribune* editor Gerry Kern pulled his team together to find ways to re-engage with their audience after years of declining readership and competition from digital platforms. Gerry and his team came up with a new initiative called Trib Nation, an effort that would seek to use multiple platforms to talk to loyal subscribers and, hopefully, attract new readership to the *Tribune*.

Tapping their inner improviser, the *Tribune*'s leaders found two great new ways to co-create with readers. The first started with a single tweet. Trib Nation manager James Janega asked a handful of *Tribune* reporters and editors if they would gather at the famed Billy Goat Tavern after work one night. (This is the Billy Goat of *SNL* fame, the place Second City alums John Belushi, Dan Aykroyd, and Bill Murray lionized with their famous sketch "Cheezeborger! Cheezeborger! No Coke. Pepsi.") Janega then sent out a tweet inviting readers to come down to the Billy Goat if they wanted to talk face-to-face with the paper's reporters and editors. When more than 100 people showed up, Trib Nation knew they might be on to something.

The second co-creation opportunity Trib Nation developed was *Chicago Live*, a novel collaboration with The Second City. Hosted by legendary *Tribune* writer Rick Kogan, *Chicago Live* was a series of live conversations between various cultural and political figures and the writers who had reported on them for the paper. We provided the theatrical support for the production, which included a director, a stage manager, and weekly satire on the news of the week, which provided the link between all the different stories presented on the stage. The shows featured a variety of guests ranging from Chicago mayor Rahm Emanuel to Cookie Monster. After each presentation, the audience was invited to stay for drinks and mingle with the show's stars in the lobby. As people found themselves in conversation with some of the most interesting figures in the city, this quickly became one of the highlights of the program.

The *Chicago Tribune* reaches more than 3 million people every day through their newspaper and digital services, but beyond the occasional letter to the editor, they were not in a two-way communication with their clientele. With Trib Nation, the *Chicago Tribune* created their own Improv Sets so they could co-create with the consumers of their product and give them the same level of engagement readers have come to expect from media platforms. They established context by moving their communication with their readers out of the newspaper and into a bar or on a stage; the change of venue and informality allowed the dialogue with their audience to become more intimate. In this more relaxed environment, the *Tribune* was also able to set and manage the expectations of their readers. The whole idea was to deepen engagement, which almost always requires a decrease in the scale and size of one's audience.

CO-CREATION SOMETIMES REQUIRES CAUTION

Whether you're co-creating on the fly or conducting more controlled Improv Sets, there are a few lessons to live by. We learned them the hard way so you wouldn't have to.

Some Words Are Funny, Until They Are Not

You have to stay abreast of changing tastes and social mores. The power and meaning behind words can change drastically over time. Right now, the word *retarded* is probably the number one instigator of outraged calls and letters to our offices. Five or ten years ago, that word could play in a scene a thousand times and no one would care. Today, audiences are far more likely to demand that the word be excised from a show. *Gay*, used as any sort of derogatory modifier, is another word that fell seriously out of vogue a few years back. We learned that lesson a few years ago when enacting an old scene from the 1980s during a tour of college campuses. The students were the first to tell us that using the word *gay* in any sort of negative context was ignorant and outdated; it needed to be sealed in the vault, along with the old racist Bugs Bunny cartoons and Disney's *Song of the South*.

Some words were never funny to begin with. How many times have we seen corporate executives, broadcasters, and celebrities blow their entire careers by using hurtful language? Steve Krieser, an executive in the Wisconsin Department of Transportation, was fired for comparing immigrants to Satan, and broadcaster Don Imus was fired for disparaging black women on a college basketball team. Often these individuals are trying to be funny. Public relations executive Justine Sacco was fired after making a "joke" about Africa and AIDS on Twitter; Gilbert Gottfried lost his gig as the voice of the Aflac duck after making tasteless tweets following the tsunami in Japan in 2011. Dan Turner, press secretary for Mississippi governor Haley Barbour, had to resign when an e-mail became public in which he made a tasteless joke in the wake of the earthquake in Japan.

God knows The Second City is one of the least politically correct environments you can work in. But that doesn't mean we don't always want to be working at the top of our intelligence. Broad communication requires that you understand the power of your own words. Leave the comedy to the professionals and engage with your own young staffers to assess the ever-changing vernacular.

Talking About Religion Means Trouble

Second City performers can scream about liberals and conservatives; make-believe shoot people onstage; explore drug use, prostitution, and war; portray all the sins and swear like a sailor on shore leave. But when we talk about religion, it's guaranteed the hate mail will come flying in.

Here's a helpful hint: Leave the religious satire to us. Don't joke about it and don't offer armchair philosophical musings on it in the business environment. Our founding fathers recognized the fundamental need for a separation of church and state. The same goes in the workplace.

Tragedy Today, Comedy Tomorrow

Dozens of hilarious Second City scenes have featured mock gunplay—so many that we train our touring companies on the proper procedures for packing a prop gun when traveling. But in the hours after the tragic Sandy Hook Elementary School shootings in Newtown, Connecticut, we cut every single scene with a gun in it. As of this writing, we haven't brought the guns back. You can't predict these kinds of disasters, but you can be responsive within your own organization to how those events might change the public perception of your ad, your product, or your services.

In the wake of 9/11, even mentioning the word *airplane* elicited gasps of horror from the audience. We took such words out of the show. Of course, we are back with plenty of airline humor now, and it was only a matter of months before some comedians returned to that familiar comic resource of bad food and cramped seating.

There is a reason that one formula for comedy is "tragedy plus time." Second City teacher Anne Libera adds that in our work, it's really "tragedy plus time plus distance." A year after the Columbine massacre in Colorado, our Second City e.t.c. cast created a piece of satire about school shootings, featuring two characters who bungled their own attempts to re-create that horror. The scene got generous laughs every night it was performed until one Saturday evening, when a young woman ran out of the theatre in tears. A college freshman at Northwestern, she had been a senior at Columbine High School when the shooting occurred. She will likely never gain enough distance from that event to make a humorous piece of satire work for her.

The lesson is that you must pay attention to your business's place in the broader conversations going on in the world. Don't inject your brand into stories and events that are unconnected to the watercooler talk. On the twelfth anniversary of 9/11, there was a firestorm about various companies posting social media content tying their brand to the remembrances of that tragedy: AT&T posted a picture of one of its smartphones showing two beams of light where the Twin Towers once stood in the New York City skyline; the backlash was so heated they quickly deleted the image and were forced to issue an apology.

In the end, there will always be risk when you let your audience in on the act, but we've learned from experience that the benefits to be had in the form of better shows and happier audiences far exceed the risks of ceding some control of the creative process. We suspect the same holds true for most businesses. Given that it's something you can try on a small scale, why not give it a whirl and see how your audience responds when you give them a chance to be part of your company's story? Just remember: Engaging in rapid co-creation works best in the ideation stage and requires you to create a safe platform where everyone knows you're just riffing and the occasional gaffe won't get anyone (or everyone) in trouble. Then, as the stakes rise, you can slow your co-creation down, taking more time to carefully shape your communication in a way that highlights your unique and authentic brand identity.

CHANGE IS HARD: COMEDY AND IMPROVISATION MAKE IT EASIER

E. B. White once wrote, "Analyzing comedy is like dissecting a frog: Few people are interested and the frog dies of it."[16] We'll keep our analysis brief, but it's important to note that we have spent multiple decades at The Second City studying how to apply humor effectively across a variety of mediums. In the course of those efforts, we've developed our own theories about comedy.

In this chapter, we'll show you how to use comedy as an invaluable and effective tool when you want or need to seize the attention of your audience, especially when your business culture is experiencing change. And while using comedy to get a foot in the door, you can use improvisation as a tool for managing internal and external business challenges, whether they are market forces or forces of Mother Nature. Further, the one-two punch of comedy and improvisation allows you to tap into something treasured by many brands: authenticity.

It's amazing that so many businesses use comedy as a means of communication, yet so few have any actual expertise in what comedy is. So what is it? We turned to our colleague Anne Libera, former executive artistic director for The Second City Training Centers, who left that gig to become director of the first college degree program in comedy writing and performance at Columbia College Chicago. She also happens to be Kelly's wife.

Rather than looking for one giant, all-encompassing theory of comedy, Anne has used her time in the trenches as a performer, director, and teacher to focus on the essential elements of comedy. She identifies three: recognition, pain, and distance.

THREE ESSENTIAL ELEMENTS OF COMEDY

1. Recognition

Anne notes, "We constantly use the element of recognition as a way of generating comedy at The Second City, from localizing content when we perform in another city, where the mere mention of an adjoining suburb elicits howls of laughter, to a simple callback, wherein the audience laughs when a character from a previous scene pops up in an unconnected scene later in the show." We see a wonderful example of comedy of recognition in a scene created on our Mainstage by Rich Talarico and Rachel Hamilton during the Monica Lewinsky scandal. The scene, set in the kitchen, began in silence, the actors communicating nonverbally. The audience laughed as they recognized the behavior of a married couple: She kept her back to him; when he approached her to touch her shoulders, she bristled. He had done something bad and wanted forgiveness. She was having none of it, choosing to give him the silent treatment instead. When Rich finally pleaded, "Hillary . . . ," in the unmistakable southern cadence of Bill Clinton, recognition hit the audience on multiple levels. The married couple onstage were also the lead players in the political scandal that was dominating every news outlet. Which brings us to the second essential element of comedy.

2. Pain

The Clinton sketch didn't get a laugh just because the audience recognized the storyline. They were momentarily startled by the discovery that there was more to the story than they originally thought. They also responded on some level to the awkwardness and pain of two people dealing with marital infidelity. As Anne says, "You can't have comedy without something just a little bit uncomfortable. Even the simplest and most childish of jokes (Q: What is brown and sticky? A: A stick) contains brief discomfort due to the feeling of 'I thought I knew the answer and discovered that I was wrong.' And that stick joke has additional discomfort connected to a taboo. What do most people first think of that is brown and sticky? Mud? Or something else that we aren't supposed to talk about?" Discomfort, schadenfreude, tension, incongruity, violence, surprise, cognitive dissonance, risk, awkwardness, taboo, danger, mistakes—all of these can be painful, and all can be used to create comedy.

3. Distance

If we just pull together truth and pain we don't have a comedy, we have a tragedy. We need one more element. We need to put that truth and pain in a context that makes an audience feel safe and free to laugh. "I like to refer to this context as 'distance' because distance in time or space usually creates a level of objectivity that provides safety," notes Anne.

If a joke about a recent event bombs, comedians, knowing

that comedy is tragedy plus time, will ask their audience, "Too soon?" Physical distance also creates a safe context for comedy. Mel Brooks says that "tragedy is when I cut my finger; comedy is when you fall in a hole and die."[17] Repeated exposure to something negative results in distancing, which explains the gallows humor of soldiers in combat and doctors in emergency rooms (or colleagues in the midst of a workplace debacle).

Safe context isn't just about distance; it can also be familiarity or trust. Risky jokes are funnier when told by someone whose good intentions have been established. You might laugh at a taboo situation in a room full of friends but feel uncomfortable laughing if your mother joins the circle.

At The Second City, we write our shows in front of an audience, which gives us ample opportunity to adjust each of these three elements over the creation process (note how Mick Napier found a way to create a safe context for the audience to enjoy the Superman scene in the previous chapter) and develop our understanding of how to apply that knowledge in all sorts of situations outside our theatres.

In the corporate work we do through Second City Works, we're always striking the balance between what's funny and what's over the top. It's natural, almost axiomatic, to think of large corporations as change averse, humorless, and too reverent of their products, history, and leaders. But we're here to tell you that our government and not-for-profit clients can be even tighter when it comes to calling out the truth through comedy. Those folks might have better benefits than the average Joe, or the satisfaction of working for a good cause, but they're dead serious about their work, and they generally don't like to take any crap from us.

That's why it was so gratifying for us to be brought into some important work being done by the U.S. Department of Education, which was convening a conference on education reform with the three constituencies vital to that effort: school board presidents, school superintendents, and teachers' union leaders. (Now you government spending watchdogs out there, put down your pitchforks. Our work at the conference was funded by a private donation, not by taxpayers.) A key to that effort was getting all parties to honestly acknowledge the challenges everyone in the system was facing and to recognize how their own contributions and actions could help or hinder reform efforts. The thinking was that, for change to come, everyone had at least to be on the same page regarding the current conditions of the public education system.

Sound like fun? Actually it was, because our clients at the D.O.E. knew the value of using humor to call out problems and barriers in a truthful, constructive way.

And instead of lampooning the unions, school boards, or superintendents, we did what any self-respecting comedy troupe would do: We aimed our comedy at people not in the room and found a common enemy.

In this, case, we chose Finland. Seriously.

Through a cleverly written opening sketch that we performed live on the conference stage, we took on the popular but somewhat unsubstantiated idea that the Finns had it all figured out when it comes to education. The sketch was funny, and not because we wore wigs, spoke with Finnish accents, or made reindeer jokes, though we did all those things. It was funny to this mixed group because it highlighted an idea (a misconception?) that had been drummed into all their heads: Our education system is irredeemably broken and the Finns can run circles around us.

The sketch did what all good comedy does: unite people by holding a mirror up to the situation and forcing the audience to understand a shared truth. In this case, the truth was that there's real work to be done in education reform, no outsider has a perfect system, and no insider has all the right answers. It was risky for the D.O.E. to encourage these disparate, often antagonistic groups to laugh in the face of a tough challenge, but in doing so they were able to show that there was room for agreement and incentive for common action. Over the two days we were on-site at the conference, we performed several similar scenes that served to satirize the existing assumptions and arguments that have dominated educational policies for decades. And while we can't say that we single-handedly changed the course of public education in the United States, the feedback we got in the moment and after the fact confirmed that we helped make this conference less contentious and more productive than it might have been had a less upbeat tone been set from the top.

Mission accomplished.

The One-Two Punch of Comedy and Improv

Change is hard whether you work in education, politics, a start-up, or a Fortune 500 company. And while we're not a change management consultancy, we know from our work with literally thousands of change-averse companies that comedy and improv can play an important role in affecting organizational transformation. When the status quo is no longer working, organizations and leaders need a way to change the conversation and get people to reconsider the assumptions that are leading them astray. There are different ways to do this, but we help our clients do it with thoughtfully crafted comedic messages that grab people's attention and get them to face the uncomfortable reality of the situation, without being threatening or disparaging. Comedy makes it possible to talk gently but forcefully about what's broken, while clearly making the case for change.

But popping the tension bubble around an organization's failings and challenges isn't enough. It doesn't help anyone to just do a comedy drive-by and make fun of people's serious problems. To be truly effective, we have to help our clients build the capacity to solve those problems. So when people are afraid to push into new territory or to adopt major change, we bring in our secret weapon—improvisation—to help them build the key skills that improve individual and organizational agility, thus enabling and supporting whatever change the organization is making.

Said another way, we've learned that comedy and improv form a powerful one-two punch that makes change easier. Comedy makes it possible to identify and talk honestly about problems, and improv builds the key skills people need to deal with the problems that come with any enterprise-wide change agenda. We'll provide some concrete examples of that, starting first with the comedy side of things, then bridging later into the improv side, when we'll offer some tools, tips, and exercises that you can do on your own to increase your team's capability for positive change.

CALLING OUT THE ELEPHANT

In business and in life, before you can get people to change their behavior, they have to change their attitudes, and before they can change their attitudes, they have to understand there's a situation that needs to be viewed differently. We've seen this play out in our clients' boardrooms, call centers, and break rooms, but one of the best examples we've seen of this principle in action occurred not in a business setting but on board the ships of our long-standing partner, Norwegian Cruise Line.

Our partnership with Norwegian is unlikely and fascinating.

It was Andrew Alexander's idea. He saw an article in *USA Today* that talked about how the cruise industry was starting to branch out and work with a variety of different brands. Broadway musicals, Oxford University, Las Vegas revues—all were taking steps toward providing branded entertainment content on cruise ships. And he thought, why not us?

Our highly sophisticated new business development team got to work on this right away. In other words, we googled the top five cruise lines and sent them a letter and a brochure saying they should call us.

It worked.

Within weeks we had set up face-to-face meetings with three of the leading cruise lines. A month later, we made a deal with Norwegian Cruise Line to bring a Second City ensemble on board the *Norwegian Dawn*. The cast would perform both scripted and improvised shows, and we would also do improv workshops for anyone who wanted to try it.

We sensed that we had just opened up a fantastic business and talent development opportunity (and in fact, three members of the cast of *Saturday Night Live* ultimately cut their teeth on Norwegian Cruise Line ships: Vanessa Bayer, Aidy Bryant, and Cecily Strong), but we did have initial concerns about the appropriateness of our brand and how it would play for those audiences. The kind of searing political satire that is our bread and butter on our stages in Chicago and Toronto was not going to be our go-to material on a cruise ship. Essentially, we had to replicate the model for how we develop the shows for our resident stages and apply it to this whole new stage—which meant we let the audience tell us what did and didn't work.

Without the benefit of a lot of trial and error, we made many educated guesses as to what content would work best, and we were able to swap material in and out as we started performing on the ship. The first shows were largely made up of some of our greatest hits—scenes from the archives that have stood the test of time. But what came next was a bit of a surprise.

What happens when you stick a bunch of improvisers on a cruise ship? They start writing material about living on a cruise ship. And thus the ensembles unwittingly discovered The Second City's key creative contribution to the world of cruise ship entertainment: making fun of absolutely everything about the experience. And the best part was that Norwegian Cruise Line did not flinch. Quite the opposite—they encouraged us to go further and deeper with our satiric lens. Nothing was off-limits, and to their credit, that remains true to this day. After nearly ten years together, The Second City has full-time ensembles aboard six Norwegian Cruise Line ships. In that time, we have employed 450 actors, musicians, and directors to work solely with Norwegian.

There is power in allowing yourself to look foolish. There is power in addressing the elephant in the room that comes with any cruise experience on any cruise line. We take on the tiny cabins, the long lines at the buffet, the never-ending ship-wide announcements blaring over the loudspeakers, the toilets that have such a powerful flush you feel your whole body being sucked into the bowels of the ship. And the audience eats it up.

One of the biggest challenges for the staff of a cruise ship is bad weather. While the cruise line has no control over the elements, the ship's passengers do not pay thousands of dollars to be holed up in their tiny cabins while the rain is pounding and the waves are swaying the ship with increasing strength. It upsets everyone.

In bad weather, the theatres are usually full. When this happens, we're in the unenviable position of performing our comedy show for 2,000 people ranging from mildly grumpy to all-out angry. Some people might think the best approach would be to make sure the last thing we do is mention the weather. Why bring up the very thing everyone is so upset about? We do the opposite.

We don't stop mentioning it. If the elephant in the room is the weather, you can be sure we're going to make a lot of jokes about the weather. And it works. Throughout the course of the show, you can feel the tension bubble getting smaller and smaller. We give the audience a vehicle for releasing the negative energy they are feeling at the moment. When people can laugh at their problems, they diffuse the emotional part of the issue. We respect the audience's attitude about the weather, but we don't revere it, because that would eliminate our ability to improve the situation with laughter.

So what does our Norwegian Cruise Line experience have to do with organizational change? We see an important connection. In most corporate change initiatives, it's a foregone conclusion that at least some people are going to be pissed off that they have to change something, whether it's their reporting structure, their day-to-day duties, the systems they work on, or even the way they're compensated. Just as cruisers are nauseated and grumpy when buffeted by unexpected rain and high seas, so are employees who are being forced to change in ways they didn't anticipate. Too often in these situations, we see companies spend a lot of time, money, and energy downplaying the change, as if they can persuade people that the changes being imposed aren't that hard. We call this being "business candid," which is our variation on the term *business casual*. Just as business casual is about 85 percent comfortable and a little fraudulent, so is business candid. People who try to be business candid would be better off leaning in to the conflict and calling it out truthfully and thoughtfully, thus giving their people a chance to process it more quickly so they can move on.

Remember what we said at the top of the chapter: Change initiatives require real behavior changes, and before people can change behaviors, they have to change their attitudes. Defusing the tension with comedy is one great way to get people to change their attitudes more quickly so you can get on with the real gains that come with effective transformation.

WHO PUT MY ETHICS IN YOUR COMPLIANCE?

OK, we know what some of you are saying right now: "Yeah, all that comedy theory is great for you Second City schmucks, but it would *never* work in my company. We're more conservative than the Tea Party, and our boss would never let us laugh openly at real problems."

Well, make yourselves cozy, friends, this part of the chapter is just for you. We wrote a little song with you in mind, and it goes like this . . .

Actually, we don't know how to write songs, but we are über confident on this topic. We've faced your skepticism a thousand times, and while it's legit to be concerned about how something will play inside your company, we know from experience that when you need to convey an important message, there's not a company or topic that can't benefit from the thoughtful use of comedy. And we'll go further: the more critical the message, the more you actually need comedy to cut through the clutter, grab attention, and make the issue safe to talk about. Counterintuitively, the higher the stakes, the more you need to create space for honest conversation, and few things do that better than comedy.

Still not sure? What if we told you that we've quickly but stealthily revolutionized the field of corporate ethics and compliance training over the past three years by bringing comedy to the thorniest, dullest, get-it-wrong-and-you-might-go-to-jail topics? We've done just that, and with all due respect to our partners in compliance, this was a field that was in desperate need of change. For those of you who've ever had the misfortune of slaving through an e-learning course on insider trading or the Foreign Corrupt Practices Act, you know how boring—and sometimes insulting to your intelligence—this content can be, with mind-numbing training, offensive role plays, and a "check-the-box" approach that rarely drives positive behavior change, but does usually breed cynicism among the poor souls who have to endure the annual code of conduct certification.

Of all our work with corporate clients, ethics and compliance training has to be the biggest comedic dead zone. Traditionally, that's where funny goes to die. Even by the somewhat soft standards of corporate comedy, this stuff is brutal. That's why we took it on, and shockingly enough, it's become a huge hit for our business. The quick and dirty story is that after the financial crisis of 2007, Second City Works was looking for some recession-proof lines of business, since our staple activities in corporate entertainment, training, and marketing were in the tank. Then we got a couple of assignments to make engaging videos promoting a company's ethics hotline or code of conduct, and in digging into it, it occurred to us that here was a good business opportunity. Big companies are obligated to do this training, and the products in the market were almost universally despised. So we developed a library of video content called RealBiz Shorts: "shorts" as in short funny videos, and "real" in the sense that we were calling out the lameness of most existing compliance training. We were keeping it real.

Three years and almost 300 blue-chip clients later, RealBiz Shorts is a huge business for us, and it's predicated on this counterintuitive idea: the higher the stakes, the more you can benefit from comedy. We've been successful not because we've made fun of illegal or unethical behavior, but because we're making hard-to-understand topics relevant and interesting to the average employee, thereby making it more likely that they'll pay attention in the first place.

So, to honor comedy's rule of three, we'll offer our mantra on the role of comedy in business communications with one small addition: You can't change behaviors until you change attitudes, and you can't change attitudes until people are paying attention. The comedic approach we use in RealBiz Shorts gets people to pay attention, and the positive changes we've seen in the compliance field suggest that everybody is the better for it.

The Respect/Revere Dynamic

When companies (and individuals, for that matter) lack a sense of humor, we often find that it's rooted in the mistaken belief that one must remain reverent to institutions and ideas. We think differently. We offer to replace the word *revere* with *respect*.

A quick visit to www.dictionary.com gives the following two definitions:

RESPECT: Esteem for or a sense of the worth or excellence of a person, a personal quality or ability.

REVERE: To regard with respect tinged with awe; venerate.[18]

We heartily endorse respect. We urge caution at reverence. Here's the difference: Respect is like the rules of the road—

it's how we're constantly not crashing into each other at intersections. Respect demands that you consider the other.

Reverence, however, turns respect into a thing so perfect that it can't be touched.

Respect allows for dialogue between individuals who may think and feel differently, thus creating a path for potential understanding and change.

Reverence makes idolatry of individuals and institutions. It speaks *to* us rather than *with* us. Reverence is the enemy of change.

This dichotomy is constantly playing out in business, in politics, and in our religious and educational institutions. Any paradigm that embraces a hierarchical structure—which is just about every institutional pod we shift between—has a respect/revere dynamic at every level of its organization:

> Worker and Boss
> Constituent and Representative
> Laity and Clergy
> Student and Teacher, Teacher and Principal, Teacher's
>   Union and School Boards.

Because each of these relationships involves people holding different status, it's easy for the dynamic of mutual respect to shift into one of reverence. When that happens, the person of lower status feels unable to call out the foibles and imperfections of the higher-status person or the institutions that person represents. And in any setting, being afraid to speak truth to power makes it hard to effect change when it needs to come. Since the time of the court jester, and probably even before that, in some cave somewhere, comedy has served to level the playing field and give people of lower status a voice with which to call out the failings and inadequacies of their leaders.

At the heart of the very best satire is the ability to maintain a respectful disposition while being earnestly irreverent. That's how it makes people think, which opens up the possibility for change. People don't hear you when they don't feel respected. When The Second City is hitting it out of the ballpark, you can bet nine times out of ten that we are walking the line between respect and irreverence like a tightrope. This is our bread and butter. Perhaps the most radical yet underappreciated aspect of The Second City is our ability to find perfect balance between two seemingly dissimilar things: our gift for satire and, with it, our ability to shred what needs to be shredded; equal to that is our devotion to the idea of Yes, And, which is ultimately about affirming and building on ideas that already exist. We tear down, but we also build back up to create something better, more magical and more insightful than what existed before.

Make no mistake: If you're too reverent toward your product or service when embarking on innovation, you'll be too timid to take on substantial change. You'll love what exists more than the possibility of creating something better.

Why is this so important?

Because almost every act of innovation—from product design to advanced pedagogy to putting together a winning baseball team—occurs in the face of changing the status quo. Innovators question facts. Innovators are restless when it comes to the truth. For example:

> Albert Einstein—respected the fundamental laws
> of math and physics, but didn't revere Newton's
> Law so much that he wasn't compelled to prove
> new and different relationships between natural
> phenomena that better explained how the universe
> works.

Steve Jobs—respected what technology could do to improve people's lives, but wasn't so reverential to the status quo that he couldn't see room for improving the aesthetics and usability of technology for the nontechnologist.

Billy Beane—the Major League Baseball general manager made famous in Michael Lewis's book *Moneyball* (and the hit movie of the same name)— respected the budget parameters of the league and the Oakland A's owners; nevertheless, he completely revolutionized how teams use statistical data to compete more effectively within those parameters.

These innovators and change agents were really improvisers, using Yes, And, along with the same respectful irreverence that we use to create our works of satire, to change the world for the better.

It's easy to embrace these ideas when you're the agent of change doing God's work, against all odds, because other people got things wrong. They're going to have to change, damn it, so you can make your dysfunctional company work a little better. But what happens when you're on the receiving end of the change mandate, and people think it's you who is unwittingly standing in the way of progress? Whether the topic is a company strategy, an internal policy, or a new product development idea, you, as leader, have to be willing to listen and stay open to the possibility of a better way, and show your own balance of respect and reverence. You're not off the hook just because you're not CEO. You may not be *the* leader, but if you manage others or have responsibilities that can help or hinder the work of a broader team, you're certainly a leader, which means we're probably talking to you.

THE LOOKING GLASS

We try to set a tone of respectful but irreverent leadership at The Second City. If we're being honest, though, we know that we sometimes get it right and often get it wrong. Whatever the case, we know that once a year, come hell or high water, we're going to hear the unvarnished truth from our staff at our annual holiday party, which we call, ironically enough, The Second City holiday party.

For decades, a main feature of Second City's holiday party has been the staff show. It's a roughly forty-minute revue put on by the night and part-time day staff of the theatre, often using scenes from current revues to parody the experience of working offstage and out of the limelight at The Second City.

It's impolite, vulgar, barbed, unapologetic, hilarious, and so, so true. And no one is exempt.

From the star players on the stage to the division bosses to the company owner, the staff pulls no punches in exposing any minor issues of vanity, unpopular business decisions, and even, as was the case only a few years ago, a comic plea for insurance from part-time employees that was as pointedly serious as it was scathingly uproarious.

It began innocently enough with a song pointing out the differences between the full-time staff who worked during the day and the nighttime staff who did all the dirty work. It led to a waitress from the night staff walking offstage to stand directly in front of owner Andrew Alexander's seat, while singing to him that "he could dress up a pair of jeans, so why can't he get us insurance?" And although general manager Mike Conway had buried himself under his table, cringing at what may have been the most provocative act on that stage in recent memory—given the personal implications for those involved—Andrew was laughing. And he was thinking. The next day, he asked that the team immediately investigate a way that we could offer insurance to everyone in the building. And we did.

The night staff was able to use comedy to bring about change not only because their satire was respectful (it was entirely appropriate to our culture), but also because it was effectively irreverent, calling out a widely held concern about health insurance in an open forum, in a funny, honest way.

Of course, we know that most companies don't produce stage shows for the annual holiday party, but there are lots of ways to create a culture that is appropriately loose and irreverent.

- One of our professional services clients issues an internal newsletter featuring senior management bloopers from throughout the year, to make it safe to identify screwups.
- The project management company Basecamp conducts product roasts to point out design and production flaws so they can take what they have learned and apply it toward improvements.[19]
- More and more companies conduct regular "if we could do anything" ideation sessions to give people a forum to share out-of-the-box thinking.

Maybe your organization already does its own variation on this theme. The specific prescription isn't important. What's key is that leaders create an environment and conduct rituals that gently and respectfully force imperfections, mistakes, and disagreements into the open. Positive organizational change can't come in an environment where fear of retribution means that problems are swept under the rug.

RESPECT, REVERENCE, AND AUTHENTICITY

Aside from improving your organization's capacity for positive change and innovation, there's another important dividend that comes when you get the respect/revere dynamic right: authenticity.

Authenticity has always been prized. Business leaders want to be regarded as authentic. Politicians do. Brands want it, too. These days, however, there seems to be more talk about authenticity than in previous decades, perhaps because the web, for all its failings, forces greater transparency and openness. In a world where everyone with a web connection has a megaphone and isn't afraid to use it, company flaws and bad corporate citizenship inevitably come to light. So do good deeds, success stories, and thank-you notes.

What it all boils down to is this: Thanks to the web, organizations can't hide from the audiences and customers they serve, and that new reality is forcing transparency, candor, and, in some cases, irreverence that would never have been seen before.

For example, just look at Andrew Mason's letter announcing his departure from Groupon:

- -

People of Groupon,

After four and a half intense and wonderful years as CEO of Groupon, I've decided that I'd like to spend more time with my family. Just kidding—I was fired today. If you're wondering why . . . you haven't been paying attention. From controversial metrics in our S1 to our material weakness to two quarters of missing our own expectations and a stock price that's hovering

around one quarter of our listing price, the events of the last year
and a half speak for themselves. As CEO, I am accountable.[20]

- -

It's probably worth mentioning that Mason was a familiar figure around Chicago's Second City and, under his tenure,
Groupon was well known for hiring improvisers for their humor
as well as their adaptability and quick thinking.

But other companies have taken the same tack. Domino's saw a
significant jump in its revenues when it created a campaign around
the fact that its pizza wasn't really very good, going so far as to
offer money-back guarantees to anyone who didn't like the new
and improved pizza. You could make the case that Domino's irreverence (admitting to subpar taste is unheard of in food advertising
where "bite and smile" shots and gorgeous vegetables tumbling in
slow motion are the norm) was the ultimate sign of respect for
their customers, because it spoke the truth they experienced.

When Netflix changed its policies and increased its fees, CEO
Reed Hastings took the heat, said he was sorry, and returned to
the previous policies. Today, Netflix is riding a wave of success
on quality content such as *House of Cards*, *Arrested Development*,
and *Orange Is the New Black*. Hastings wasn't so reverential of his
position and his company's policy that he couldn't see the virtue
in reversing course and respecting the wishes of his customer base.

Here, one last example to explore the relationship between
respect, reverence, and authenticity:

We get hate mail at The Second City. But the difference
between our company and your company is that we're likely to
frame that hate mail and put in on display in our lobby for every
customer to see.

We do this for two reasons: The first is that it's funny; the
second is that it reinforces an essence of the brand that is impor-

tant for the audience to understand prior to seeing a Second City show. It shows audiences, authentically, who we are. And frankly, we display that mail on the wall because it is just as important to reinforce The Second City brand essence for our own staff on a daily basis. And to us, it's a lot more authentic than some un-contextualized slogan of empowerment hanging over the doorway of the company break room.

So if you're hoping to change or innovate, you need to be able and willing to tear at the existing power base—to risk offending those who are inextricably married to the way things are currently done—and have the confidence and moxie to build up something completely new in its place (and eventually have the fortitude to cope when the next innovator comes along and does the same thing to you). When we get hate mail, it tells us we're doing something right and that we are being true to ourselves. However, other organizations that don't deal in such subversive products as ours might double-check their strategy if they receive a deluge of true hate mail and start hemorrhaging customers. But if you implement change and no one complains, chances are you probably didn't go far enough.

Being authentic while toeing the line between respect and irreverence isn't easy, and it's probably why most people just assume that change agents and innovators are born with a special gene that facilitates their success. But the reality is, you can train people to become better innovators and agents of change. We do it every day.

IMPROVISATION: A WAY TO BUILD CHANGE SKILLS

After many years and a wide range of experience with different kinds of clients, we have found that improv is a great way to build skills related to change and innovation. We train literally tens of thousands of people every year in improvisation, and while many of them are aspiring actors, a large percentage of the people we reach through Second City Works are business professionals working in teams who are looking to sharpen some aspect of their job performance. What we do varies assignment by assignment, but we tend to focus on team agility, trust and support, and open communication. Here we'll explore these one by one.

Team Agility

There are many advantages to working in big organizations, but one of the disadvantages is that they tend to be slow-moving, change-averse, and lacking in organizational agility. On the other hand, good improvisers are, by definition, very agile, with the ability to think on their feet and respond to new information with great skill. So it makes sense that we have something to offer teams when it comes to being nimble.

We once worked with a consumer technology company that was struggling to get products through their pipeline and into the market in a timely way. They were big and global, a market leader, but the larger they got, the more they seemed to get bound up in the product development process. They needed to find a way to be more nimble and adaptive to market conditions so they could better compete against the newer, more agile competitors that were entering the market. One project manager summed up his challenge well. "We all know that our process is complex, but one of the biggest issues we face is keeping project momentum when unexpected changes happen, which is often."

As part of a larger change management initiative, the company's learning and development people engaged us, and together we created a series of change and adaptability workshops for the key players in the process, largely from engineering, supply chain, project management, sales, and product marketing.

Within the larger change workshop we created, we included an exercise called Take That Back to help team members become more flexible in dealing with the unexpected and to encourage them to take the initiative to bring about new and useful solutions when they occur. The exercise is performed in groups of three. Two people are instructed to have a conversation about anything at all; the third person's job is to be a human buzzer of sorts, randomly stopping the conversation with a clap, at which time the person speaking has to take back the last line of dialogue she spoke and replace it with something new that also fits the flow of the conversation. One group's Take That Back conversation went like this:

PERSON 1   On my way to work today, I was dropping my son off at day care when I saw an accident.
PERSON 2   I always feel awful when I come across an accident, because I'm afraid someone got hurt.

CLAP

PERSON 2   I always feel awful when I come across an accident, because I know it'll make me late for work.

CLAP

PERSON 2   I always feel awful when I come across an accident, because it reminds me of how I totaled my dad's car when I was sixteen.

This kind of conversation was happening simultaneously in other groups within the workshop and, after a while, we stopped for a debriefing. We talked about what it took to be successful in that unusual kind of conversation. One of the participants said, "I thought it was going to be harder . . . and I was really surprised how well my teammates adapted on the fly and came up with new thoughts to keep things moving forward."

For this group, and so many others we work with, it comes as a great relief to know that they and their teammates are more resourceful than they think, and that if they keep the right frame of mind, they can almost always come up with solutions when roadblocks emerge. Often, the biggest stress inducer within teams isn't the change itself, it's the personal responsibility we feel to adapt successfully to change and not let down the people around us. Take That Back is an exercise that reminds us that we have everything we need to cope with the unexpected if we trust ourselves and turn to one another for help in solving the problems that will inevitably arise.

We did several of these workshops over the course of a year with this client, touching several hundred key employees along the way, and we watched them struggle and continue to improve their new product development process. They still have challenges, to be sure, but overall product development stays on time and they hit their deadlines with much more reliability than in the past. We can't say that our contribution was the key driver in their improvement, given that we were just a small part of the initiative, but we can say that the people who left our workshops felt genuinely better about their individual and team agility when they finished their sessions with us.

One workshop participant summed it up well: "We work in an engineering environment that is all about eliminating defects and imperfections," she said. "But since people are imperfect, things won't always go according to plan, and now we're in a better position to adapt to the unexpected bumps in the road that come with any product development process."

Trust and Support

Because change usually involves everyone in the enterprise, it's important to establish an environment of trust and support when you're working through a large-scale change initiative. There's usually more friction, confusion, and tension when things are changing, and knowing you can trust the folks around you is key if you want to succeed. That's always tough in large organizations, not because people are inherently untrustworthy, but because we often have different priorities and agendas. Even when we want to support each other, we don't think to do so because we're so focused on dealing with our own responsibilities.

The Canadian arm of Second City Works was hired to help a large retailer several years ago that was embarking on a significant organizational restructuring. Accompanying that initiative was a series of systems and process changes that represented a pretty radical departure from business as usual for the company. We were brought in about a year after the restructuring, and by that point, some of the initial trauma had passed. But some residual pain lingered, and there was the perception that the reorganization had created winners and losers in the company.

We were asked to work with the leadership team, a group of about fifty executives who represented different functional areas of the company. The goal was to help them reestablish the mutual trust that had gone missing after the restructuring and create a more cohesive operating unit. We did a series of things to support this effort, including a fun and funny executive talk show that allowed members of the leadership team to explain the reasoning for and benefits of the changes the company had undertaken. The change workshop we did with the execs was perhaps the most important part of our work with the company.

By their very nature, all of our improv workshops have a

team-building aspect. They're fun and lively, and people get to interact in a very different way than they typically do on the job. But beyond general team building, we wanted to run some exercises with these folks that would get to the heart of their trust issues, to show them viscerally and experientially what trust is and how it feels when it's missing.

To do that, after a series of warm-up and general communications exercises, we ran a routine called Thank You Statues. In this exercise, the team forms a circle. One brave person is asked to step into the center of the circle and strike any pose he likes (goofy or straitlaced, it doesn't matter). Once he strikes a pose, someone from the outer circle has to come to the center, tap the first person out, and assume his own pose. When the second person taps the first one out, the latter says "thank you" and then rejoins the circle.

We let this exercise go on for a while. There were some awkward pauses when nobody wanted to venture into the center, because posing in front of your peers is a little weird and, for more modest people, somewhat intimidating. But after several rounds, we asked people to pick up the pace, and before long, things were really moving. We concluded the exercise with a twist—we no longer had people tap each other out or say thank you; we just had them enter and build on the poses of their peers inside the circle. And at the very end, we asked the last two people in the circle to name the two statues. One was "Curling, Not Your Hair"; the other, "Date Night at the Birdbath." Who knew the Canadians had such an abstractionist streak in them?

After we named the statues, the group gave themselves a raucous round of applause, and we stopped to talk about the exercise.

"Man, that was hard to step in and put myself out there," said one guy. Another responded with, "I got all caught up in my head trying to figure out something cool to do, and in the meantime, left you out there hanging in the breeze."

Thank You Statues is a great exercise because it embodies what we all do on the job every day. We put our ideas out there for judgment. We get, or don't get, support from our teammates. Some of us get bogged down in coming up with our own version of the coolest thing, all the while ignoring the thing that needs support right in front of us. And others help our colleagues out when they're in a bind and need support.

Having gone through so much organizational disruption, these executives needed to be reminded how much they depended upon each other to be successful, no matter what the reorg had done to their roles or relationships. They needed to feel again how risky it could be to initiate an idea and how good it felt to be supported by others when they did. They needed to remember that any change is manageable if you go into it with a spirit of gratitude and collaboration. We broke for lunch right after Statues and the group leader came over to our lead instructor. "So this is interesting," he noted, looking at the different groups of executives sharing lunch. "None of them are sitting with their usual groups." Laughing, he pointed across the room. "Those two guys eating lunch together? I never thought I'd see that happen."

Open Communication

The third area where improv can support organizational change is in creating more open communication. Think about it. If you've ever gone through a major systems implementation or company reorganization—any substantial change initiative—you know there are going to be glitches that even the best planning can't anticipate. In these situations, frequent, open, and honest communication is critical to make sure problems are identified and solutions worked out quickly and efficiently.

One of the central benefits of improv is that it teaches people to be more open-minded, and this open-mindedness is usually what's needed to troubleshoot problems that arise with change.

One improv exercise we incorporate into change leadership sessions is Emotional Option, or Emo Op for those in the know. Emo Op is generally regarded as a performance game in improv circles, but it can be an interesting choice in training programs as well.

It's simple to do. People pair up and talk about anything at all. At various points, our instructor will shout out an emotion—angry! giddy! somber! worried!—and the pairs must continue their conversation in the tone of that emotion. Imagine how that might play out if you happen to be having a conversation about fly-fishing or popcorn. The key here is to teach individuals that the content of their speech will change simply by attaching an emotion to the way in which the words are delivered. They can be the exact same words, but they mean completely different things when said through the filters of different emotions.

There are several ways Emo Op can help you deal with change better. First, it sharpens your ability to read and recognize the different emotions people express in conversation. Second, you can determine if you want to match that tone or find a different one that'll help you achieve what you want. Third, it's an important reminder that communication is more than the words you speak.

The inevitability of change in business and in life simply means that we will be continually subject to all sorts of challenges and dilemmas. But comedy makes change more manageable, opening the door for all kinds of conversations. Once that door is open, an expertise in improvisation can make that conversation a whole lot easier to have.

USING FAILURE

There's a reason the late-night Improv Sets that follow our scripted shows are free: There's a good chance a lot of them will suck; they'll simply fail. We're OK with that. In fact, while our business is unique, failing is one thing we have in common with literally every other organization on the planet. We fail a lot. Sometimes spectacularly. We do it on our stages, in our conference rooms, on the road, when we hire and fire people, and in our training centers. We failed fifty-five years ago, we fail today, and we'll certainly fail tomorrow. That's what happens when you understand that the key to staying relevant in the world is constantly challenging and reinventing yourself.

OUR FAMOUS FAILURES

Here are a few of our failures, in all their glory:

We Are Not Foodies: A new menu item, the Royster Oyster,

was introduced at the restaurant we once ran in Toronto—it was a hamburger with an oyster on top. As the ambulances lined up to take dozens of customers retching from food poisoning to the hospital, it became clear the dish should be removed from the menu.

How Not to Open a Theatre: We were weeks away from opening a new theatre in Cleveland, but since contracts hadn't been completed, we decided it was wiser to postpone any preopening traditions such as advertising, group sales, or promotion. Interestingly, the seats did not magically fill up once the ink hit the paper. Then, when we finally presented our first revue, *Burning Riverdance*, we received a cease-and-desist letter from the internationally renowned Irish dance company, forcing us to change the title and all our artwork. The few audience members who did show up greeted almost every satiric barb about the Bush administration with a resounding "Boooooooooo!" Nineteen months later we closed. Yay!

That Worked, So This Will Too: On the heels of our highly successful training video series on ethics and compliance issues in the workplace, we saw a vast fortune to be made on the topic of sales training. Unfortunately, when developing our first batch of videos, we overestimated the appetite of our buyers for funny communications about the sales cycle, and also overspent on product development . . . by a lot. Hollywood had *Ishtar, Waterworld*, and *John Carter*. We had this. On the bright side, we're cautiously optimistic that the project will break even before we both retire.

Second City Montreal: We've announced the opening of a permanent Second City theatre in Montreal three different times over the last twenty years. To date, we have never opened a theatre in Montreal.

Serious Improv: In the mid '90s, a small group of us—

including Adam McKay (*Anchorman*, *Funny or Die*) and Brian Stack (*Conan*)—decided that we would rent out a storefront theatre near Wrigley Field to present an evening of improvisation. This time, though, we weren't going to improvise for laughs. The show, *Invisible Rails*, was not going to be comic. Rather, our actors would improvise strictly dramatic scenarios. No one ever said improv always had to be funny.

Sound pretentious? It was. Sound like a dreadful way to spend an hour in the theatre? You bet. One favorite moment was when Del Close, a much-revered Second City alum and teacher, showed up to a performance. Just as the house lights began to dim he found out that the show was going to be dramatic improv . . . which propelled him from his seat and out of the theatre just as the stage lights were ascending.

Avant-Garde or Dumb: Del Close directed a show in the late 1980s that would end up being his last at The Second City. Given his stature, Del was given free rein on all design elements for the show, which included the hiring of a couple he knew to create a mural onstage as part of the set design. The first sign we might be in trouble came when the couple—both wearing protective masks—started spray painting the walls in the theatre while their unmasked, sleeping baby lay in her car seat not ten feet away. The second was that evening, when the mural was unveiled and we saw there was a giant cow painted on one wall and a spider on the other—neither of which had anything to do with the material in the show.

SEE? THAT DIDN'T HURT A BIT . . .

Despite our many failures, our company is rightfully regarded as a big success that has had far-reaching, positive impact in the entertainment world and brightened the lives of the millions of people who've laughed at our shows and learned in our classrooms. We know that failure is not something to be feared; in fact, it's something to embrace. That's why we spend a lot of time trying to encourage our clients to get over their fear of failure—it stops too many would-be innovators cold in their tracks.

No matter what you do for a living, you're going to fail at some point. Politicians fail. Student counselors fail. Salespeople fail. Bankers fail. Placekickers fail (and sometimes cost one of us a lot of money). The thing is, if you're good at what you do, you're going to fail, because it means you're out there taking risks. As people who have failed will often attest, failing isn't that bad; it's the fear of failure that can be paralyzing. That's what keeps less successful people up at night, causing them to disengage, to hold back and not commit their full energies to their companies and coworkers. It causes them to quit a difficult task, refuse a promotion, avoid their boss, or hold their tongue in meetings. Fear of failure drains companies of their innovative lifeblood. Organizations that accept failure as a natural part of the creative process, however, can see tremendous increases in productivity, morale, and innovation, so it's worthwhile for managers to figure out how to create a safe environment where their ensembles won't be afraid to let loose. It's not enough just to tell people it's OK to fail and hang a bunch of posters emblazoned with platitudes; you have to model fearlessness.

We've talked a lot here about how one shouldn't work out of fear and how fear manifests itself in various ways that negate success. But the biggest fear is that of failure. So how do companies model such fearlessness? First, employers need to create low-risk opportunities for their employees to try stuff out or, in other words, fail. Risk taking is not everyone's favorite activity, but if you want your employees to pursue new and different ideas, they need to know that their job isn't on the line every time they take a shot and miss. Lower the stakes a bit and see what happens.

Chicago-based software company Basecamp gets this very well; it makes a popular project management app by the same name, and company executives wanted to create a work environment where employees were empowered to call out flaws in product design without fearing retribution or just seeming too negative.[21] So, at a company-wide meeting, they blew the dust off the old comedy convention of the celebrity roast and created their own "product roast" to identify the failings of the products under development. By their own admission, the execs found it very enlightening. Team members felt OK about pointing out problems and flaws because the roast created a safe context for people to speak up. *Heck, it was expected of them.* And, just as in the good old days of the Dean Martin celebrity roasts, everyone got to take a shot, though in this case, they probably did much less smoking and drinking in the process. While these developers, designers, and project managers never thought they'd be channeling Don Rickles or Foster Brooks when they got into app development, they appreciated the roast for giving them some fun with their small-scale failures and a place to gather ideas in order to improve their products. As happy users of their software and proponents of using comedy to improve business, we raise our martini glasses in Basecamp's general direction.

Besides creating safe spaces to fail, you should also consider providing platforms—as Second City does with its Improv Sets—that promote experimentation and reward those who think outside the box. If the platform doesn't exist, new ideas and new voices will never break through.

One of the most glaring examples of an industry that lost a

valuable platform for experimentation is terrestrial radio. Years ago, it was during the overnight shift at radio stations when you would hear the youngest DJs doing some of the most interesting programming. They played new and unusual artists, and the banter was looser, edgier, and far more improvisational. But with the advent of automated content, along with the quest to cut costs and monetize every inch of radio real estate, the overnight shift gave way to prerecorded disc jockeys and paid infomercials. Without a place for young talent to experiment, terrestrial radio has lost its venue to build distinctive, interesting, and new voices, ceding the creative edge to podcasts and satellite radio, which both contain relatively low-stakes opportunities for inventive programming. While terrestrial radio is still looking for the next Howard Stern, a host of exciting, alternative voices have come out of the podcast world. Marc Maron was a struggling comedian who started interviewing other comics in his garage. By December 2013, his podcast *WTF* had over a million downloads, and he's gone from playing small comedy clubs for a couple thousand dollars a week to starring in his own television show and playing in 500-plus-seat theatres for more than $20,000 a week. We know this because we tried to book him at our UP Comedy Club (280 seats) for a week of shows and his agent turned us down. Ultimately, any company that desires its talent to work out the bugs on a new product needs a small, safe platform where experimentation—which includes failure—can occur.

Additionally, both managers and workers need to banish the thought that failure is a zero-sum game. It isn't. Failure is always present—sometimes in doses larger than we like, but more often in the tiny little failures that are a part of everyday activity. Shifting your mind-set to accommodate failure in the creative process is essential to making it a positive part of your workflow instead of a barrier.

OH, HOW WE FAIL:
LET US COUNT THE WAYS

We think The Second City is a perfect model of fearlessness. In fact, we regularly fail in six distinctive ways, which can be instructive to anyone, no matter their line of work. We list those at the end of the chapter. First, though, why do we fail?

WE FAIL IN ORDER TO CREATE

To improvise is to create something out of nothing, in the moment. At Second City, we do it in front of an audience. When that's what you do for a living, you're essentially getting paid to present your rough drafts to a few hundred people in a crowded room. More accurately, you're getting paid to let people watch you evolve your rough drafts into something brilliant, unexpected, and funny. It's a glorious thing to watch. Make no mistake, though—it can also be extremely messy.

When we are creating a Second City revue, we fiddle with just about every dial imaginable, all in the name of developing the best material and building the best show possible over a ten-to-twelve-week process. We fiddle with characters, dialogue, the order of scenes, and the score. We do this, with full knowledge that our tinkering may cause our preview audience short-term pain (in the form of scenes and sometimes full shows that miss the mark), in order to achieve longer-term gain (in the form of a revue that can run successfully for many months).

During rehearsals and preview performances for the 2010 Second City e.t.c. revue *The Absolute Best Friggin' Time of Your Life*, actress Christina Anthony and actor Tom Flanigan were testing out a scene wherein a white nurse was in conflict with a black doctor. The twist was that an African American actress was playing the Caucasian nurse, and a Caucasian actor was playing the African American doctor.

Great, daring idea, right? Unfortunately, when the scene hit the stage, it was clear that the audience was not on board with what we were trying to do. Every night the actors tried the scene in the Improv Set, they were met with stony silence, so much so that after the third time they did it, the director's assistant remarked, "You know, this is supposed to be a comedy show."

Sometimes, you have to accumulate a series of failures in order to finally succeed. In this case, the actors realized that they needed to make the audience laugh earlier so that the race of the actors onstage became incidental to the scene's content. Each time they went back onstage, the actors added more laugh lines to the scene until they could feel themselves winning over the audience. That scene, "Raisin," became one of the most talked-about scenes in one of the most successful revues in the modern era of The Second City.

Director Billy Bungeroth noted, "Four of us were creating that scene—myself, Tom, Christina, and the audience." That's something important to remember when you are part of any team that is tasked with creating a new product: When you get the client's feedback in the process of creation, you create with a decided advantage.

Most organizations say they want to innovate, to advance, to push the envelope, but few are willing to do that if it means going back to the drawing board as a matter of regular practice, and fewer invite their customers to pay them for the chance to watch their products crash and burn. Most organizations would rather sidestep the hard stuff and focus on what has worked in the past. Certainly, this approach is understandable—companies can't continually risk it all on new ventures. But increasingly, the companies that thrive, from Walmart to Cisco, IBM to Pinterest, are those that embrace disruptive innovation in at least part of their product portfolio. Especially for the legacy brands, the tendency not to rest on their laurels but to focus on new ways to do better or do different is key to their longevity.

ONE STORY, TWO FAILURES, A BIG SUCCESS

In 2012 the opera star Renée Fleming attended The Second City e.t.c. production *Sky's the Limit: Weather Permitting*. Ms. Fleming was in town in her role as creative consultant for Lyric Opera. As she was enjoying the production, she heard a distinctive sound: her own voice. The talented musical director, Jesse Case, had included a recording of Ms. Fleming in the revue's score.

When Ms. Fleming approached Jesse after the show, he was afraid she was about to threaten a lawsuit. Instead, she said, "I have an idea . . ."

Within a few weeks, a creative and producing team from The Second City was sitting across the table from a group at Lyric Opera Chicago, including Renée Fleming, Alexandra Day, Lyric's director of PR, and Lyric's general director, Anthony Freud, brainstorming ways that these two iconic Chicago institutions could work together.

Improbable doesn't even begin to describe the situation.

Divas and divos versus ensembles; 3,563 seats versus 300; an art form that is expansive in every single way versus an art form in which brevity and subtlety are core. But the force of Renée Fleming's vision and Anthony Freud's keen instinct, combined with Second City's absolute willingness to try anything, provided the groundwork for an evening of opera-influenced comedy that would serve as a one-of-a-kind gala called *The Second City Guide to the Opera.* The show would feature original scenes and songs about all things opera, from *The Ring Cycle* to master classes to the lonely life of a single musician in the pit.

In this case, we had one night to get it right—which meant we had to create nights where we could get it wrong.

A month or so before the show's debut, we took over one of the late-night improvisational sets in our brand-new UP Comedy Club in Piper's Alley in Chicago. We told the audience that had just seen one of our scripted shows that they could stick around for some untried material that we were creating for our new show with Lyric Opera. Members of The Second City's team, along with Lyric Opera's team, were in attendance. Later, when we asked Alexandra Day, Lyric's director of public relations, how the night went, she answered by relating what her colleague Drew Landmesser had said during the drive home: "Well, maybe other people will find it funny."

Of course that wasn't what we wanted to hear, but for Second City folks who are trained to take failure in stride, this was simply a marker in the road to creating something wholly new. We suspected there were a few reasons the material bombed: The audience that night was not necessarily made up of opera fans; it was late; and something was just not clicking onstage. We also knew that most of the material wasn't up to snuff yet. We would need to throw some parts away, rewrite others, and continue the process of refining and honing the work. So we didn't panic.

Luckily, our partners at Lyric Opera were open to the creative process. Anthony Freud said as much in a television interview: "The moment we lose the ability to take risk, the confidence to take risk, is the start of artistic death."[22] We all knew how important it was to create a safe environment for the creative team to work in if they were to produce compelling content. So we didn't intervene. We didn't replace the director. We didn't have a big serious meeting outlining the consequences if this show were to fail. We simply acknowledged our collective understanding that the material hadn't come together yet, and we let the actors, writers, and director do their jobs to fix it.

Things got more intense. Ms. Fleming had recruited her friend Patrick Stewart—that is, Sir Patrick Stewart of *Star Trek* and *X-Men* fame, not to mention countless acclaimed theatrical roles, and the recipient of many of the theatre world's highest honors—to join the production. Both arrived the day before the show to rehearse the handful of scenes that had been written specifically for them. It's not unusual for us to have limited rehearsal time with the various guest stars who perform with us on occasion for private shows, fund-raisers, and galas. But the stakes were a little higher this time.

Let's set the scene as these two legends arrive at the rehearsal room in the Civic Opera House: The show is sold out—so sold out that Lyric Opera covers the pit so that folding chairs can be brought in to accommodate more spectators. Press interest in the show is huge. We have made television appearances, been featured in print articles, and the blogosphere is running full tilt, with most bloggers wondering why this collaboration is happening in the first place. The two stars of the night have less than twenty-four hours to be worked into a two-act revue. And the last public workshop is a disaster.

But then, two things happened prior to the show that gave both parties hope that everything might just be all right. The Second City cast for the production included a number of actors who had also worked for the Improvised Shakespeare Company, an extremely gifted group that comically improvised full-length Shakespearean plays. So we had the idea to see if Patrick Stewart might agree to improvise with the ensemble in addition to the few scripted scenes that we had sent him in the weeks prior. As

Sir Patrick sat in the rehearsal room, the cast interviewed one of the production assistants, asking him about his workday, the general things he liked and didn't like. From there, they improvised for ten minutes—brilliantly. "So you just made all of that up?" Sir Patrick asked, adding quickly, "You're mad." He agreed to do it. So that was the first thing.

The next thing occurred during a laborious run-through of the material just hours before the doors opened. We were performing the closing number. It sounded great. The whole cast was lined up with Renée and Sir Patrick, singing about the joys of living in Opera Land. Renée's communications director, Paul Batsel, who was watching the run-through, whispered to Kelly, "They just did *La Bohème*. They can make it snow right then. Why not pull out all the stops?" It was a great idea. We ran up to director Billy Bungeroth, who just smiled and said to the technical crew, "Hey, guys? Think we could get some snow right there at the end?" This could never happen at our theatre on Wells Street in Chicago.

As the finale ended that evening, with the "snow" drifting down on the ensemble, the audience leapt to their feet in one of the loudest and longest standing ovations any of us had ever experienced. At least from The Second City's end—we're pretty sure this was de rigueur for Renée and Sir Patrick.

Writing in the *Chicago Tribune*, John von Rhein summed up the evening: "The first and most obvious question to be asked of *The Second City Guide to the Opera* was: Was it funny enough to meet the expectations surrounding this unlikely match-up of Chicago's world-renowned comedy troupe and just as renowned opera company, Lyric Opera? You betcha."

Most important, von Rhein added: "The script—by Kate James, Timothy Sniffen, and musical director Jesse Case—had been worked and reworked in a series of public tryouts at the UP Comedy Club and elsewhere. The refining process showed: Belly laughs flowed as readily as naughty vulgarities, the likes of which have seldom if ever been uttered on this venerable stage."[23]

While it's unlikely that your next work assignment will align you with a world-class soprano and a master thespian, the model is the same: When creating wholly original products there will be many failures along the way, making it an absolute priority that you plan for those failures to occur in ways that won't put the entire enterprise at risk.

The stigma of failure—especially in business—is so prevalent that few take the time to examine the properties of failure. But if you really parse it out, you can find ways to make the parts of that failing work toward an eventual success.

Look at your business: What are the parts that make up a failure in your line of work? If a new product doesn't sell well, what were the steps along the way in the design of the product and its marketing strategy that may have contributed to its not selling? Did enough attention get paid to beta testing the product itself and its marketing? Could there have been an advantage to more actively poking holes in the product or trying out a handful of other promotional plays in getting people to buy into what you are trying to sell?

Understanding failure can give you the tools to use it to your advantage. Since we have a lot of experience in this area, we've identified six ways that we choose to fail in the course of our business that can work for you, too.

THE SIX WAYS WE CHOOSE TO FAIL

We Fail in Public

While nobody likes to fail, people are much more willing to fail quietly and privately than flame out in front of others. Studies show time and again that one of the greatest fears people have in life is of public speaking, probably because they panic at the thought of being judged and because of the public nature of such a failure. The anonymity of the Internet has turned many forums into online free-for-alls of opinion, pontification, and vitriol, but in the real world of business and life, where we are easily recognized, people spend a lot of time purposely in the shadows, afraid to make any kind of open, public contribution that could invite the scrutiny of others. It's not that people lack ideas, commitment, or capability; it's that they are controlled and held back by the fear of public judgment, specifically the judgment that their ideas aren't good enough. Yet it's critical that they get over this fear, because while the instinct to avoid failure is natural, it doesn't help us grow. It doesn't allow us to experience the opportunities that build up our confidence by putting us in situations where we see that we can actually succeed.

Believe it or not, we get it. Even though we're out onstage creating something out of nothing seven nights a week, we don't like to fail any more than anyone else. We've just learned to put failure in proper perspective and that where there's a chance of public failure, there's also a chance of public acclaim. We focus on that, and people outside the theatre would be wise to do so too.

Here's something that people who don't make it their life's work to fail in public should remember, and that might make it easier to take the leap and try failing a little more often: Oddly enough, while our society is quick to judge others and criticize failures, we also are willing to reward those who jump back in the saddle after epic failures. Whether it's presidents, athletes, or pop culture stars, we love to build famous people up so we can knock them down, and the bigger the blow-up, the better. Only then, once we've confirmed that the public figure is as flawed and human as we are, are we willing to grant them a second term or a second chance, or put them on reality TV. The private sector can take a cue from the public fascination with a good tale of redemption. When those in charge demystify failure, it opens up the opportunity for increased creative output among individuals who no longer feel the need to simply play it safe.

We Fail Together

History is replete with inspiring examples of the lone inventor, struggling against the odds, persevering in the face of withering criticism, creating something unimaginably wonderful only after all hope has been lost. We love individual geniuses, and we agree with the late, great adman David Ogilvy, who once said, "Search the parks in all the cities, you'll find no statues of committees."[24]

But when it comes to improvisation and creating new material, we put our full faith in ensembles at The Second City, for all the reasons we outlined in Chapter Two: They speed up the creation process, they generate more good material, they're flexible, they actually enable the growth of individual stars . . . and most important, they provide the creative safety net that allows individual cast members to risk and flourish.

One tenet we take extremely seriously at The Second City is "always take care of your partner." It means that we take great care to support our cast members, not judge them. It means we work together, onstage and off. Onstage, it also means that you don't leave your fellow actor hanging—don't let him fail if you can help it. In corporate culture, it means that you need to support your employees as whole individuals, not widgets. Businesses that do this will build far more effective staffs and increase retention. Your support can be anything from providing employee development training, to extending or supplementing an employee's particular skill set, to small acts such as remembering birthdays and publicly acknowledging individual successes.

For workers, having the backs of their fellow employees is equally vital. When support, trust, and respect are a given in your place of business, you have set the table for invention. Come to the aid of a coworker who may be flailing in a meeting; take ten minutes each day to visit the offices of individuals in other departments; when you screw up, say you're sorry. It's not all big, sweeping actions. Sometimes it's the accumulation of small acts of support that provide a true sense of community inside a business.

And this is exactly the environment you need to foster if you want to encourage your ensemble members to push into difficult territory.

There is a tradition among our ensembles that in the seconds before they go onstage to perform, each cast member gives a quick hug to the other members and says, "I got your back." This happens before each and every performance. The verbal and physical cue is just one more reminder that the group empowers the individual, and vice versa. In this environment, people will be willing to risk everything in pursuit of something great.

Dick Costolo, the CEO of Twitter, in an interview with *Bloomberg Businessweek* talked about the improv ensemble as it relates to a business ensemble:

> When I first got to Chicago and was doing improvisational comedy, there was a group of folks from Ivy League schools, like Rachel Dratch, who graduated from Dartmouth. There was another group from midwestern universities, the Chris Farley types, who were like, "We are going to swear onstage and take our shirts off." There was a fascinating balance there. It created a great blend of intellectual comedy and slapstick.

That's exactly the mix you want to foster in a company. On one hand, you have your innovators. These are your dropouts and visionaries. They say, "I need the freedom to think about this problem outside the limits of whatever constraints other people might operate under." They tend to think holistically about solutions. Then there are your Stanford graduates with their 4.0 grade point averages. They're disciplined. They think in terms of measuring themselves and everyone around them with data. You want both to make it all work.[25]

When you think about the biggest challenges in your business or organization, challenges that will require bold action and some risk, are you likely to develop solutions as an ensemble or to approach the problem as a collection of individuals? What we've observed in our work at The Second City and with our corporate clients is that people are more willing to contribute fully if they know that risk can be shared among the many. Furthermore, they learn that the "failures" of their ideas are really only temporary shortcomings that can be fixed when combined with the ideas of their ensemble mates. One great example comes from Farmers Insurance, which has been a terrific client of ours for many years. One of the reasons we respect our Farmers friends so much is that they are willing to break the mold when it comes to creating internal communications and training programs. They regularly consult with us to develop comedic training videos to help their claims reps improve customer service. Our clients don't just roll the dice thoughtlessly and hope for the best. The programs we develop with them touch more than 10,000 people, and the stakes are high. Our clients know that if they're going to take creative risks that'll ultimately make their training more interesting, memorable, and effective, they're also going to have to invest in thoughtful instructional design and get the full support of their internal customers. Before any major Second City/

Farmers production receives the green light, we take great pains to enlist all the key stakeholders in creative brainstorming and ideation. This goes far beyond the standard corporate approval processes, which tend to focus on covering your ass and sharing only the bare minimum to get the needed blessing. Our work with Farmers stakeholders is truly ensemble building, where we focus on *what might be* with a given program, involving dozens of people in the ideation and creative work.

The end results are programs that routinely win awards in the training industry, lift customer satisfaction, and delight the legions of claims reps who don't have to endure the typical indoctrination that is, unfortunately, standard in the industry. In fact, our productions look more suitable for TV than the training room, and the reason we're able to do out-of-the-box work is that we've built a tight ensemble that reaches together to be great.

Of course, when implementing this kind of group collaboration in your organization, you want to avoid the dangers of groupthink, the dumbing down of ideas that can happen when people seek consensus. We're certainly not advocating that. Just as we at Second City answer to directors who ultimately make decisions among competing ideas within a cast, your organization or division will need a final decision maker to assure that the strongest ideas survive. Ensembles are for idea generation, where new, untried approaches can emerge and be incubated to the point where a decision must be made.

We Fail Fast

Speed is an essential part of our game. Improvisers are usually extremely quick-witted and nimble, able to think on their feet and adapt seamlessly to changing environments or circumstances. Their ability to listen and react intelligently and comically is what separates great improvisers from people on the street.

Our need for speed also ensures that when the inevitable failures happen, we move quickly on to the next new idea without stressing over what was wrong with the previous one. We know that there will be time later on to deliberate over what didn't work. At that moment, however, we can't let failure derail us because we've still got a show to finish. Humor is the great equalizer in this regard. In an improvisational set, when a scene fails and the actor onstage is able to say something like, "well, that happened," actors and audience alike are able to laugh at the thing that didn't work and immediately move on. By simply acknowledging the failure with a quick joke, that failure's power has been instantly dissipated.

The same can be done in the workplace. Sometimes it's as simple and spontaneous as inviting everyone out for happy hour to commiserate and decompress after a tough day, and sometimes it can be more planned and elaborate. Tom once worked at the advertising firm Ogilvy & Mather, where for years he and a colleague presented mock awards for "career-endangering stunts" at the annual holiday party. In truth, the stunts were rarely career endangering, but the shared experience of watching the company's "blooper reel" of screwups and misadventures for the year was cathartic for many. More recently, Tom had a hard time delivering a taped conference invitation on camera. Try as he might, he botched take after take, and with each blown take, his blood pressure rose and his off-camera vocabulary got saltier. His crackerjack video crew saw the opportunity to make lemonade out of their boss's lemons, as it were. They pulled together, with great relish, an outtake reel of Tom screwing up and losing his shit on camera, and saved that video gold for a company retreat, where they shared it with colleagues and their unsuspecting boss. Nobody was fired for making that outtake reel, and everyone laughed their asses off because the execs had created a work environment that accommodated and laughed at the day-to-day failings we all experience.

Let's be clear: We're not suggesting that every failure be celebrated, because there are times when failures can have huge consequences that cause real harm to companies, employees, and customers. What we're saying is that, in any work environment, imperfect people—i.e., everyone—will screw up, and if you can maintain an open and healthy attitude about your imperfections, you'll get higher employee morale, more engaged staff, and an organization that is more willing to reach for greatness instead of holding back out of fear of making a mistake. Laughing at minor mistakes and well-intentioned screwups helps create a high performance culture where that kind of greatness is possible.

In our work with business teams, we notice too much real-time Monday-morning quarterbacking, way too much second-guessing while teams are in the middle of ideation or problem-solving sessions. If they'd only wait till Monday to begin quarterbacking, solutions would come a lot easier. We're not advocating giving up critical analysis or decisive decision making. Rather, just as there is a time and a place to choose an action—to say yes or to say no—there is also a time and place to allow for the free exchange of ideas, unburdened by the need to measure quality. If you can create an environment where new ideas are allowed to flourish, even for a matter of minutes, you just might find a gem of a concept that simply needed a little time in the light to fully realize itself. At worst, you will have given the creative voices in your company that chance to freely exchange their own initiations without the stern eye of judgment on them.

Failing fast exists in a variety of industries beyond our world of improvisation, particularly in businesses that continuously seek invention and reinvention.

Jeremy Jackson is a lead technician at a technology company

called Method. In a post for the blog Co.Design, which explores design, innovation, and business, he writes: "Rapid prototyping is the process of quickly building the main feature paths of an interface. One of the largest benefits of prototypes is that they provide an easy way to get your idea in front of potential end-users and key client stakeholders. Getting the idea out of the designer's head and into a demonstrable format is an effective process for eliminating initial shortcomings and misplaced design assumptions."[26]

In the most cutting-edge restaurants, both the product (the food) and the process (the presentation) are constantly being deconstructed, reinterpreted, and reimagined. Culinary expert Matthew Robinson noted that "In the kitchen, if we fail, we fail fast, which is important for keeping the momentum of innovation up and pushing forward."[27]

In essence, the key to successfully failing fast is to allow your company and your employees to suspend judgment while in the act of creating something new.

We Fail Free of Judgment

This is crucial. No one can feel free to fail—or conversely, feel free to take risks—if they think they are being judged, either by their colleagues or their supervisors. We've already discussed how to encourage judgment-free zones within groups. But there's one more piece of advice we have for any boss or manager: Stay out of the way. Failure can be successfully harnessed only when it's allowed to exist inside a judgment-free zone.

At The Second City, once the actors and director have been cast and put into rehearsal, no one steps inside that rehearsal room unless they are invited to do so. Producers have to ask a director permission to come in on a certain night to see a preview for a show. The director is given complete control over the work, and the producer has to trust that he or she will see it when the time is right.

The creative process changes when supervisors get involved too soon. People get nervous, they want to please, they want to look good. Supervisors and managers need to understand that when they enter the room, the dynamics in that room are going to change. If they speak, they will alter the creative process. The boss's opinion matters; the boss carries the ultimate judgment. So bosses need to know when to get out of the way and let their people do their work.

You'd be amazed at how much rehearsal goes into improv, how much actors and directors agonize over the timing of a single word, toss of the head, or a raised eyebrow. Our directors and our producers are meticulous when it comes to getting our final product precisely right. But when stirring the creative stew—as we are when in the act of creating—too-early judgment will only turn individuals from rapid co-creators into rapid deniers, and the creative team will crumble.

As discussed in Chapter One, great managers know that true power lies in knowing when to be hands-on and when to disappear; when to direct and when to listen; when to judge and when to observe; when to hold their ground and when to step back and let someone else lead; and when to say Yes, And. Failure succeeds in getting people closer to great innovation only when it is allowed to proceed unencumbered by judgment.

We Fail with Confidence

There's a long list of things we don't do well at The Second City, way longer than the list of things we do well. For example, long-term strategy has never been our strong suit, and if someone can show us how to make serious money in merchandising, we might have a job for you. Seriously. Send your résumé to Kelly tomorrow. But those things we do well, we do extraordinarily well. We've been called the Harvard of Comedy (we actually think Harvard is The Second City of Higher Education). Our alumni list is a veritable Who's Who in comedy and entertainment. We're arguably the most successful theatre in America when it comes to commercial success combined with critical acclaim. And we achieved our reputation and success by taking risks and stretching ourselves beyond the comfort zone of your run-of-the-mill arts organization.

When we screw up (which as you know happens a fair amount), we rebound fast because we bring unshakable confidence that our approach, talent, and experience will carry us through. We've worked hard to earn our pedigree, and the upshot is that our ensemble members go into every creative challenge confident that they'll be successful in the end. They are more than happy to fail because they've seen that failures can lead to success.

Often, when we are starting a client engagement and getting to know our client's organization, we'll tell them about ourselves and ask some questions about them, to get at the heart of who they are so we can tailor our recommendations thoughtfully. In these situations, we look beyond the nuts and bolts and probe into the company's culture, asking questions such as:

- Is your culture a confident one and, if so, where does your confidence originate?
- What does your organization draw on when it needs to innovate?
- Is there a culture of creativity and innovation within the company that people rally around and believe in?
- Has the organization ever had to tear down some existential threat, or has it been relatively smooth sailing for the business?

Getting answers to these questions helps us infer the organization's appetite for risk and failure, and it gives us a better sense of where we may apply some of what we've learned from our own company's failures to help them.

We Fail Incrementally

Remember the improv axiom, bring a brick, not a cathedral? This adage suggests that the best improvisers don't feel compelled to bring wholly formed, finished ideas into an improvised scene. Rather, they know that the ensemble, working together, will ultimately create the full scene, so an individual's responsibility is only to bring the next idea or piece of information that can advance the scene. Because of this, no one actor carries the burden of creation, and because improvised scenes are built one brick at a time as it were, no single idea is critical, and the scene can grow into something great even if individual contributions along the way aren't spot on or interesting. In fact, the best scenes make good use of both great and seemingly bad ideas.

In business and in life, people would be far better off if they viewed their ideas not as finished thoughts to be judged, but simply as a bridge to better ideas, thoughts that grease the wheel and facilitate the contributions of others. If people lowered the burden on themselves in this way, they'd recognize that the only way to fail in this context is to withhold a contribution in the first place.

It's a counterintuitive thing that most employees don't grasp: Their ideas are critical, not because they're brilliant, wholly formed pearls of wisdom. *They're critical because they encourage the flow of ideas from others.*

Too often, people assume—wrongly—that every idea is a higher-stakes idea than it really is. They believe the cost of being wrong is just too high, or they hold back their ideas in order to protect the team from one that could slow them down or hurt the organization. This better-safe-than-sorry approach is usually not something that happens on a conscious level. We learn it by experience, by watching too many of our peers suffer the consequences of sticking their necks out. We need to start building organizations that break this cycle and show people the positive consequences of taking risk.

LAUGHING IN THE FACE OF FAILURE BECAUSE WE FAIL IN THE FACE OF LAUGHTER

In the end, we've developed a pretty healthy attitude about our failures because it's hardwired into our process and into the product we sell. In our work (and we'd submit, in yours) imperfection is more interesting than perfection. It's certainly funnier, anyway.

We don't think there's a magic formula to teaching organizations to fail well. Some people and some companies will always be more comfortable with failure than others. We do know, however, that our approach lets us work fast, take more risk, respond more nimbly, and have more fun than many other arts organizations and corporate clients, and we think it makes us better suited for the fast-changing business climate we're all in. We owe a huge part of our current success to the many specific failures we've suffered in the past, and the positive can-do spirit that comes from aiming for innovation instead of instant perfection during the creative process. Fail early and often, and you'll have a much better chance of achieving the ultimate goal—a perfect final product. As Winston Churchill once said, "Success is not final, failure is not fatal; it is the courage to continue that counts."[28]

FOLLOW THE
FOLLOWER

Improv comedy, meet Peter Drucker.

One of Second City's failures was an attempt to create an on-going product specifically tailored for Jewish audiences, *Jewsical the Musical*. The revue played a handful of Jewish Community Centers and never really found its full creative or commercial life. However, in its initial development we crossed paths with Hal Lewis, CEO of the Spertus Institute for Jewish Learning and Leadership in Chicago. When we were looking to launch *Jewsical*, we discussed the idea of debuting the show at the Institute, while also offering workshops in improvisation. After watching one of our workshops, Hal pointed out that "part of what I see you teaching is directly in line with Drucker's theories on leadership in the modern world." And when we looked more closely, we saw that he was right.

The "Drucker" Hal was referring to was, of course, Peter Drucker, the Austrian-born management consultant and author who championed a new way to look at how companies are structured. He believed that the information age demanded that hierarchical corporate structures needed to be replaced by "flatter" structures with a focus on knowledge workers. Drucker believed that companies should treat their workers as assets, not liabilities. He put a focus on the customer, without whom there would be no business. He thought workers needed more control over their work environment, and he championed the role of teams working autonomously within businesses.

The parallels to improv abound.

1. The Second City's greatest asset is its talent.
2. We give our performers and directors their own space and complete control over their creative process until they are ready to ask for our feedback and contributions.
3. Our performers' work is directly linked to the consumer—in this case, our audience—who actively participates in its creation.

Ultimately, when implementing an ensemble-first approach to your business, you are challenging the business world's perceptions of what leadership is. As Drucker put it, "Leadership is not a magnetic personality that can just as well be a glib tongue. It is not 'making friends and influencing people.' That is flattery. Leadership is lifting a person's vision to higher sights, the raising of a person's performance to a higher standard, the building of a personality beyond its normal limitations."[29] You may have a bigger title, office, or nameplate on your door, but you are still only one part of a much larger organism.

Drucker made these observations back in 1973, but by then The Second City had long known about the power of the ensemble, the role of the individual within the group, and that the old hierarchies were destined to give way to new models of management and leadership.

The following year, Drucker wrote:

> The leaders who work most effectively, it seems to me, never say *I*. And that's not because they have trained themselves not to say *I*. They don't think *I*. They think *we*; they think *team*. They understand their job to be to make the team function. They accept responsibility and don't sidestep it: *We* gets the credit. This is what creates trust, what enables you to get the task done.[30]

Once again, what Drucker identified as a new business model was something that improvisers had known for a long time. And he was right—great leaders know that there is no *I* in team. However, we disagree that effective leaders haven't made a concerted effort to banish the pronoun from their lips. They probably have. It's not an easy thing to do; even we who provide leadership at The Second City have spent the better parts of our careers attempting to remove the *I* from our active vocabulary at the workplace. It takes training and practice.

One great way to understand what can be accomplished when we abide by Drucker's laws of great leadership—trusting the ensemble, working in synchrony, taking the *I* out of team—is through an exercise developed by Viola Spolin, mother of improv theatre, called Follow the Follower.

It works like this: A group of individuals sit in a circle facing each other. On a facilitator's cue, each individual starts making sounds and movements. However, at the same time, each person is also to mimic the sounds and movements of others. No one leads, and no one follows—everyone in the group is constantly shifting their attention to see what the other group members are doing. If one person decides to shake his head, the whole group will shake their heads. However, when done right, an outsider would not be able to identify the original head-shaker. It's as though the group is in a total mind-meld, able to anticipate the slightest change in direction with all the precision and instantaneity of a school of fish. The leading and the following are constantly in flux.

The exercise demands intense focus and listening. Participants have to remain in the moment, and be acutely aware of not just what the person directly across from them is doing, but also what someone perhaps just outside their field of vision is doing. Sometimes the result borders on chaos; sometimes the group mirrors itself so well all the individuals morph into one smoothly working organism. More often than not, the group will develop a pattern of coordinated movement and sound that makes them resemble a machine, a wave, or a storm. Even when we're stripped of our status and given no direction, we humans are often able to cobble together some kind of order and form to make things work.

Follow the Follower is the physical embodiment of the change dynamic that is already in play in our office and in the greater marketplace. Change is the one constant. Successful leaders are keenly aware of this and that it is their responsibility to anticipate those changes. But how can you anticipate a variety of moving targets without the benefit of *Matrix*-like abilities to bend and twist in very cool slow motion? The contemporary leader is likely to have the qualities of the best improvisers: a deep grounding in the rules of engagement, the ability to surrender those rules in the moment, and the instinct to react in real time to all the various forces at play in the business world.

GET OUT OF THE WAY

Very few businesses have a manual for being the Boss. At least, we never got one. But we did have the benefit of receiving some pretty good advice from those who came before us.

One of the most succinct and valuable pieces of leadership advice that Andrew Alexander gave us was that we should create an environment in which people could do their work, hire the best and most complementary personnel that we could, and then allow those people to do their work without ongoing interference or distraction.

Actually, what he really said was, "Build the right sandbox, hire the right people, and get the hell out of the way."

Either way, we took his advice to heart, and it has served us well.

At Second City, the boss doesn't sit in on rehearsals. The producers who oversee the live productions check in on the shows when the director indicates that it's a good time to do so. As we explained in the previous chapter, the cast and the director are allowed to work unencumbered by outside eyes or the real-time judgments of anyone not directly involved with the actual work—in this case, creating original comedic revues. That's how the creative process should be allowed to work in other organizations, too. When a team is assigned to build new business plans or brainstorm a new advertising campaign, leaders and managers should set parameters, and then go away. The parameters are important, however. Most businesses don't have the luxury of unlimited development time. Create timelines and schedules that everyone feels can be met; make sure the group has all the resources they need to get the task done; do find time to check in during the process to make sure that the team knows that they have outside support *when they need it*, not as an everyday intrusion.

This is because when you're tasked with developing something original and creative, everyone needs some time to develop ideas free of their bosses' gaze. Getting outside feedback or judgment too soon changes the creative dynamic of the group—usually not for the better. People start worrying about whether they are responding appropriately to their managers' notes or try to second-guess what the boss really wants, instead of just letting their creative freak flag fly and seeing where it takes them. There is a time and place for managers and supervisors to enter the equation and play their parts in the process. In our case, the director of the show lets the producer know which specific night he or she would be welcome to come and give notes on the show that is in development. The producer never makes surprise "gotcha" visits. This gives the director the freedom to take risks or test new material out without fear of judgment. For example, a director might decide to purposely put up material that is bound to fail because a cast member is extremely tied to it and refuses to allow it to be cut. But when actors are given a chance to see the material fail for themselves in front of an audience, they are usually able to emotionally detach and objectively recognize that it needs to go. By letting subpar material onstage, the director gets to avoid playing the heavy, he keeps up the morale and integrity of the ensemble by making sure the actors know their ideas are taken seriously, and he ensures that there are no lingering resentments or suspicions that if just given the chance, the dud material would have worked. Still, that would be the wrong night for a producer to see the show.

It's the director's job to keep harmony intact among the ensemble members while creating first-class content for the stage. The dynamic will constantly shift in the room as some actors are emboldened and others feel down and vulnerable. At any given time, those roles will reverse. Only the people in that room who are working on the show night and day truly understand the total dynamic that is in play. It is a lot to handle, but the gifted directors at The Second City are skilled at monitoring the needs of both the individuals and the group as a whole.

Follow the Follower speaks to leaders and the led alike. It acts as a counterweight to the black-or-white, my-way-or-the-highway approach to life so many of us live. We have a natural tendency toward absolutism that is becoming increasingly reinforced by the way our media scream at us about politics and in the way that social media tends to judge first and ask questions later. The fact is, there is a whole lot of gray in the real world if you're willing to see it. If improvisation supports your ability to react in real time to changes, Follow the Follower asks that you consider the perspective of others as well, also in real time.

Lest you think we at The Second City are immune to the bad decisions that strictly hierarchical decision making produces, think again. We've hired and fired too rashly; we've initiated shows and product lines that never had a chance of succeeding; and we've made the same mistakes over and over again—which is the definition of insanity.

But we have also recognized that those poor decisions all had a common root: They were made in a vacuum. We hope that we're learning from our mistakes. Recently, we considered altering the way our seating and ticketing is done at The Second City. Since we've rarely made changes to that system over the last decade or so, it occurred to us that we might want to take an improvisational approach to figuring out if and how we might make that change.

For the longest time, The Second City was a two-price ticket—you paid a little more on weekends—but the seating was all general admission. In theory, the earlier you got here the better your seats. But one of the disadvantages of working someplace for a long time is that you adopt beliefs about the way things work in your business that become untrue over time, and because you've been there so long, you don't see the changes. In our case, we thought of ourselves as a completely democratic entertainment venue—everyone paid the same price (albeit more on weekends) and anyone could get a great seat if they showed up early. But things had changed. First of all, we were no longer two prices. Over the years, we had accumulated a number of ways in which different customers might be paying different prices for the same ticketed experience: group rates, student rates, discounted passes, last-minute half-price tickets, complimentary tickets, not to mention our introduction of Premium Seating—a small number of the best seats that you could reserve in advance. For one evening, we counted eleven different prices. The realization that we were making decisions under the incorrect belief that we had a single ticket price was, to say the least, a bit of a revelation. What came next was really a blow.

Our relationship with Columbia College Chicago is a long and varied one. Sheldon Patinkin, who still provides artistic consultation for The Second City, chaired the Theatre Department for years, Andrew Alexander sits on the board of directors, and we are partners with the college in our Comedy Studies program. We trade a lot of information with that school, and that's how Philippe Ravanas found himself in Kelly's office one afternoon, just an hour or so after we had a meeting about the ticket pricing and theatre seating. A native of France, Philippe is an arts management expert who logged executive time at Euro Disney and Christie's auction house before moving to Chicago to chair the Business & Entrepreneurship Department at Columbia College. Philippe and his colleague Joe Bogdan were writing a case study on Second City for an arts magazine. In the course of the conversation, Kelly told Philippe about the discussions we had been having and, serendipitously, Philippe had recently completed an entire case study on that very topic for another Chicago theatre. Philippe agreed to observe our seating, talk to staff, and then give us his observations.

To provide some frame of reference for the "culture" around the seating of a Second City show, you need to know only that when Kelly was trained as a host for the theatre (the person who seats the customers), his mentor was a senior host whose approach to customer service had earned him the nickname Chainsaw. To be totally fair, Second City customer service had improved a lot since then. The staff is awesome—friendly and considerate—and the managers make huge efforts to provide a great evening for the audience. But all of us were walking around with the belief that we worked at a theatre that was first come, first served; that our audience was as much blue collar as white collar; and that the number one reason anyone was coming to the theatre was to see the show (the Second City brand being that strong). It took Philippe just a few hours of impartial observation to suggest to us that some of our basic presuppositions of how our business works were just wrong.

Our "first come, first served" seating? The democratic way in which we seated the audience? That wasn't true. First, we have a number of customers whose seats are reserved ahead of time, such as friends or business associates or media. Second, we pre-seat the groups, and each group is seated in a different section to avoid any one section's being dominated solely by group business. Third, our managers tell the hosts where to seat the individual audience members, using a variety of metrics that they have learned over the years, such as keeping tall people or big people in an area where they and the people sitting around them will be comfortable. If a customer is loud and boisterous walking in the door, the manager will seat them in an area not too close to the stage where we can get to them to keep them quiet during the show and not disrupt other audience members. Military or the family of military? They always get great seats.

While we in management were aware of pretty much all of these practices, it never changed the language that we used, nor did it sink in that our practice was decidedly not the thing we called it. In a classic case of management/worker disconnect, our house staff knew that our seating wasn't democratic—we just never thought to ask them.

The blue-collar audience we often referenced? Philippe laughed. "Your theatre's zip code is in one of the wealthiest neighborhoods in the country." It's not that blue-collar workers don't come to Second City, but the vast majority don't deposit their lunch pails at the coat check. Businessmen and -women, educators, and students dominate the room—exactly the audience you would expect at a theatrical venue in an urban metropolis. It's true that Second City's audience is a lot younger than the traditional theatre audiences you find at our major regional theatres, but that didn't make it in any way significantly more blue collar.

The real surprise came when Philippe asked us, "Why do you think people come to The Second City?" We answered this question immediately and with certainty: "To see the show that's playing that night." It seemed obvious. But Philippe had done an informal survey the night he came to the show and asked audience members the same question. Here were their answers:

"I'm on a first date."
"We're celebrating an anniversary."
"It's my birthday."
"Our company bought us tickets for closing a big deal."
"I brought friends from out of town."
"We won the tickets in a silent auction."

Not a single person's first response was that they were there to "see the show." In every case, it was an event or relationship that was the primary impetus for coming to The Second City that particular evening.

For a company that is constantly talking to the audience each night improvisationally, it was a sobering discovery to realize that we had limited our communication and that we weren't always asking the right questions.

If you embrace a Follow the Follower approach to your work, you should be able to avoid those kinds of missteps. You talk to your staff, you talk to your managers, you talk to your audience—and since the conversation is always changing, you don't stop talking.

Lesson learned.

It's important for managers to note when they get things wrong. While writing this book, we have said to each other numerous times, "If only we followed our own advice more often." Perfection is not only unlikely, it's likely unattainable. Improvisation understands this without ceding to the part of us that strives for excellence. We don't believe that any one book holds the whole truth, and there are a variety of interesting and worthwhile paths one can take when reaching for goals. But part of our whole belief in improvisation is that it is not only accepting of our imperfections, it provides prescriptions to help fix the many mistakes we make in the process of getting our job done right.

There are other theatrical lessons that we've learned when the Follow the Follower dynamic has been allowed to flourish in our business, specifically in how a boss interacts with his workers during the act of creation.

Preserving the integrity of the group is absolutely essential, which is why the Second City producer gives his notes on the show only to the director, not to the cast, unless the ensemble specifically requests it. This way, the director can filter those notes and disseminate them in a way they know will be most helpful to the team members at that particular moment.

In the seminal 2011 revue *Southside of Heaven*, director Billy Bungeroth asked the producers to come to a preview of the show, but cautioned, "You're not going to like how the show starts and I kind of need you to just let me play with it for a while to try and make it work." Indeed, just as the show began, all the power in the room went out. Of course, the power outage was planned. It wasn't a funny or insightful bit, it didn't connect with the theme of the show, and it created an awkward moment that killed all the momentum the show had gained. But the director had a plan, and he just couldn't kill it off before seeing if it could work. Hence, the blackout. It was awful. Even in the dark, you could see the concern on everyone's faces in the room. The house staff was concerned because the audience was confused; the marketing director was concerned because it just looked like we were incompetent. We aren't sure how the cast felt, but it's likely some of them had just had their doubts confirmed.

Ultimately, the fake power outage gave the show exactly the kind of off-kilter jolt that the director was looking for and ended up as a weird technology call forward to one of the most ingenious pieces created on a Second City stage in the modern era. You see, while the power was seemingly out, actor Tim Robinson was vamping onstage with audience members, asking them about things that made them afraid or uncomfortable, using the only microphone that the stage manager could get to work. What no one knew was that each of these conversations was being recorded and, in turn, Julie Nichols, the musical director, was digitally adding them into a prerecorded mix. Minutes later, once the power was "fixed," the audience started hearing their own responses as part of the soundtrack for the show. The initial awkwardness of this fake power outage eventually paid off once Billy and the cast perfected the technology exchange and the audience realized that the whole thing had been planned.

Southside of Heaven became one of the great shows of the modern era in no small part because of what happens when people are willing to Follow the Follower. There was a great deal of experimentation during the process of creating the show, and without the cast's trust in the director, the director's trust in the cast, the producer's trust in the director, and, most important, the audience's trust in the whole enterprise, it would never have reached the heights that it did.

A different example of how Follow the Follower can work showed up toward the end of the second act. Actor Tim Mason has created a number of interactive pieces that make the audience an active participant in the comedy being created right in the moment. The scene he wrote is an astute response to the way technology connects us in real time and changes our perspective on privacy. In addition, it is a prime example of how by listening closely and focusing on group dynamics, a leader can reflect what he sees right back at the group, thus giving them an opportunity to objectively weigh their actions or behavior.

In this scene, Tim portrayed a seriously creepy TSA agent. It opened with him gliding across the stage in a rolling office chair, berating the audience members as if they are passengers waiting in line to go through security check at the airport. His character proclaims:

"Yeah, that's right, every time you fly we take a picture of you naked. It's for your safety. It's for your protection. And it's also for me to get my rocks off. Now you might find that a little bit scary and you might find that a little bit creepy but guess what, the world is a creepy place right now. And though I'd like to see each and every one of you naked before you fly today, I don't have the time. But that's OK because I can tell everything I need to know about somebody just by looking at them."

Tim goes on to pick out a table in the front row and guess, wrongly, where they are from and what their occupation is. He picks another table and guesses their name—he's close, it starts with the same letter. When he gets to the third table, he not only guesses their name and profession, he dredges up all sorts of intelligence on the audience member: pictures, recordings, writings. Sometimes he would recite the specific details of how they ended up at Second City that particular night. His information was all 100 percent accurate, and it would literally freak out the room each and every night the show was performed.

Here's how he did it: Prior to the show, we would identify the individuals who were to be seated in the front row for that evening's performance. A quick Google search later, we essentially assembled a dossier on each person. Thank you, Facebook.

Together, these excerpts from *Southside of Heaven* provide a twofold look into Follow the Follower. As a business, Second City needed to trust its creative teams and give them room to experiment. Remember our adage: Sometimes being a good boss means getting out of the way. Second, in both cases, the cast created material that could work only in a dynamic exchange with the audience. The reason the pieces worked was because our audience was in on the act—maybe not initially, but eventually.

The more you talk to your audience, or get to know them any way you can, the more you learn. After Tim had revealed all this deeply personal knowledge on the unsuspecting audience member, gleaned from a simple name search on the Internet, he would glide over to one more group sitting far stage left and start telling them even more intimate details about who they were and what they had for dinner—pieces of information that Tim could have known only had he been sitting with them prior to the show. When he pulled out his glasses and a Cubs hat, they realized that he was the guy sitting behind them for twenty minutes before the show started, typing into his iPhone and, unbeknownst to them, taking notes on everything they said.

We asked Tim to share some of his favorite memories from performing *Southside of Heaven* at Second City:

- There was a woman who was a "miniature knitter." That was her job. She knitted tiny sweaters for different projects, including movies. I found a behind-the-scenes documentary they did on the movie *Coraline* [in which she appears]. Julie then played the audio where she was explaining why she loved her job so much. It was such a weird profession it stuck with me forever.
- A few times I found pictures of people in various states of nakedness or in swimsuits. I would print them off backstage and hold up the pictures, because the whole point of the scene was [to illustrate the absurdity of being creeped out by the TSA agent when] you were already naked on the Internet.

Sometimes working at The Second City is like living inside one big social experiment.

At the simplest level, *Southside of Heaven* attempts to highlight the intellectual hypocrisy of an American culture that loudly bemoans any intrusion on their right to privacy while simultaneously oversharing their daily lives down to pictures of the food they are eating at any instant. But the real power of the satire is in the fact that it makes its audience a (mostly) willing participant in the activity. It's the ultimate show-don't-tell moment. The power of the theatrical act is really in the transmission of information—that moment when everyone in the room realizes that the fourth wall has been kicked down and that the rules have changed.

And they really have changed. In our day-to-day work, we are bombarded by information—sales reports, marketing reports, trends, and opportunities. With the advent of real-time information, the ability to react to said information instantly must be strengthened and worked out, like a muscle. The trained improviser is constantly using that particular muscle to take in important information and react to it right away. Just think of how much more effective you could be in your job if you could increase your ability to process and react to all the information coming at you every day.

Learning improvisation can build that muscle. And once you have learned it, you'll be amazed at where that training and muscle memory will kick in. For example, Elliott Masie has a funny story about how he Follow the Follower-ed his way through a difficult speech:

Many years ago, I showed up to give a speech, and they had confused me with somebody else. What they wanted me to talk about, I knew nothing about. I had nothing funny to say. I had nothing to say. And everybody was expecting me to talk at length about this topic. I got up there and said, "Tell me the one thing you find most confusing about *X*," *X* being whatever the topic was. I don't even remember it now, I was that unqualified to talk about it. So people shared their concerns, and I'd be like, "OK, I've got a question. Who has an answer?" And I just kept the ball rolling like that. And at the end of the hour, I got a standing ovation. And then I got four more invitations to speak on that topic.

I did what an improv person would do. I was honest. I used the music and magic of what you can do as a leader if you give yourself permission. I filled the room. And then I used their content as the content.[31]

Now, it's ridiculous to think that you would be able to lift a 200-pound weight without first practicing some regimented workout routine. And certainly, no one would expect that you could continue to lift those weights if you didn't keep yourself in shape to do so. The part of our brain that allows us to be nimble in the moment, to react in real time as events morph and change, needs just as much tending to as the muscles in our arms and legs and heart. When you improvise, you are putting your best listening into practice; you are actively engaged in empathy; you are creating and re-creating human behaviors. Put another way, you are fine-tuning the part of your brain that allows you to read a room and interpret information as you receive it.

READING THE ROOM

In one sense, Follow the Follower is about enhancing the ability to read the room. The phrase is a little trite. When you google "read the room," you are inundated with blog posts and management articles that talk about knowing how to dress for the client and getting all the information on attendees before you walk into a meeting. But the reason you want to learn to read the room is more fundamental: If you are truly engaged in the moment and you're using all your senses to really read the room, you exponentially increase the chance that the group in that room will have meaningful and effective exchanges.

Effective leaders know how to read body language, whether they are leading a conversation or are just another voice in the room. They will note when someone on their team starts sinking in his chair or looking at her phone, which tells leaders that something about an exchange has upset or disengaged the person. The effective leader won't let that moment stand, and will quickly bring individuals back into the conversation and encourage them to continue to share their thoughts so that they remain actively involved. In this way, leaders let everyone know that they are being heard and their thoughts matter, and that keeps the flow of "bricks" coming in so they can continue building toward a new and big idea.

In *The Second City Almanac of Improvisation* there is a long list of adages that have been handed down over the years at the theatre. One of these is "Leave the action onstage." What this means is that you shouldn't try to build a scene around anything that isn't actually a part of the scene. As Anne Libera writes, "Don't story tell or plan for the future. Try not to bring up the past. Try not to focus on people or animals that aren't there. It's very difficult to have a scene on what is not there in the now."[32]

What makes an improviser better onstage will also make a leader (or anyone in an organization) better in any room. Don't linger on what's not there. Instead, focus your energies on the people and space in front of you. Don't live in the imagined future. Recognize that while it's a natural reaction to fantasize about the better job across town, reveling in that fantasy won't make it true and really only serves to distract you from improving the reality that's sitting right in front of you. To read the room, you have to exist in the moment, and existing in the moment will allow you to better read the room.

There is a lot of unlearning to do when it comes to being able to truly Follow the Follower. Part of it comes from the perfectly valid distrust of committees and groupthink. But there is a difference between committees and ensembles.

Committees are absolutely stuck in hierarchy—they report to superiors and they do not comprise talent working together to create. They are deliberative. They are not active.

Ensembles are the opposite. They work in synchronicity, and while there is leadership—a coach in sports, a head researcher on a development team, a director for a theatrical show—the successful ensemble is not focused on that leader; it is focused on the action of the group itself. It's focused on the space between the active participants, on the place where the work gets done.

One business that acts as the ultimate embodiment of Follow the Follower is Twitter. It's surely no accident that Twitter's CEO, Dick Costolo, trained in improvisational comedy while living in Chicago.

TWITTER AND THE CONTEXT REMINDER

If you look at a Twitter page, the words *Followers* and *Following* are ever present on the screen. While the operational qualities of that social media platform look a lot like the web version of Follow the Follower, it's even more interesting to note that Costolo actively applies his improvisational training to the way he leads and manages his company. In an article for *Bloomberg Businessweek*, Costolo told writer Brad Stone:

A fundamental principle of improv is listening and accepting any initiation that's made on the stage. If you start improvising that you're washing the dishes, and a minute later I walk over and turn on the TV where the sink is supposed to be, the audience feels the scene's been ruined. Similarly, I want my managers to listen and respond to their employees' perceptions, not ignore them. Managers have to be open to accepting any kind of initiation. When they deny there's an issue and reflexively defend the status quo, it creates misery for people.[33]

So while Costolo brings his knowledge of improvisational leadership to his headquarters in San Francisco each day, there are other lessons to mine from the way Twitter works. In many ways, Twitter itself is a technological reflection of improvisation. It is short-form content (really, really short form), just 140 characters, which is a lot like The Second City blackout—a short, one-joke sketch that occurs throughout a Second City revue. Twitter operates in a constant dynamic where information, right or wrong, builds upon itself. It is content in motion, never becoming a final product. Improvisation, in its purest form, is the same thing. When not used to create content, improvisation takes a variety of initiations from a group of people onstage where the audience is as much watching the way the content is building as they are processing the actual content itself.

Twitter is wonderful in this regard, and it's not surprising that so many comedians have found a whole new creative outlet by engaging with that particular social network. Colin Quinn puts out purposely inflammatory tweets in an effort to squeeze comedy out of the reaction of followers who, for some reason, don't know that he's not in earnest. Patton Oswalt is able to use Twitter to mine gold out of the widest spectrum of topics. A couple of favorite tweets include "What I learned re-watching LETHAL WEAPON: brutally murdering someone is okay if there's a smooth jazz saxophone sting right after." And "The CNN news ticker at the corner of Sunset & Cahuenga is a real-time chronicle of the death of American journalism." Of course, one of the absolute best comic voices on Twitter is the satirical news outlet *The Onion*, which disseminates its hilarious mock headlines with tweets like these: "New Michael Bay Romantic Comedy To Focus On Love Story Between 2 Explosions" and "Grandiose Delusion Of Own Self-Importance Only Thing Keeping CEO Alive, Doctors Say."

There is a downside for the comic voice on Twitter, however. *The Onion* found this out most directly when they were lambasted for a tweet criticizing nine-year-old Oscar nominee Quvenzhané Wallis; and even our own alum, Stephen Colbert, got embroiled in controversy when a Comedy Central employee tweeted a single line from a larger piece of satire that had appeared on *The Colbert Report*. Extracted from the full segment, the line could have been construed as racist—even though in its original form, it was actually an attack on racism.

It's all about context.

And Twitter provides none.

Here's the point about context: It's about knowing who your audience is at any given moment. In the case of *The Onion*, they forgot Molly Ivins's vital reminder that "satire is traditionally the weapon of the powerless against the powerful." Colbert's comments were clearly satiric when presented as part of his television show, but picking out one joke, without the benefit of a setup or delivery, generated an unintentional firestorm.

Know your audience. Dick Costolo talks about making sure managers are listening to those who work for them, which is absolutely crucial. We'd also extend that advice to listening to your clients—who are a different kind of audience. What might seem like a great idea in a private office between two colleagues may not be ready to be discussed among the full team, in which case it certainly isn't ready to be broadcast to your client base.

Business leaders would do well to make sure their employees have some training in all the different platforms on which they may be communicating. Does your company talk to employees about how they are expected to discuss their work or represent their work life when using social media? Do the folks in charge of talking to the media engage in regular sessions together to hone and align their talking points? Does your company teach people the different etiquette required when talking to different audiences, whether it's boss to boss, boss to employee, or employee to customer?

Leadership is not just top-down. It's often sideways and sometimes reversed. Follow the Follower provides a template to help the best leaders pay attention at every level of communication. In your business, it's vital to find the places where you can experiment, fail, and risk. You can do this only if you understand who your audience is and how to talk to them. Follow the Follower is really about a new model for leadership.

LEADERSHIP 2.0

A leader's role is recognizing the shift from a hierarchical leadership model to a flat one; knowing when to lead, when to follow, and when to just get out of the way; and trusting your teams and talking to your audience—all while setting the context for both internal and external communication. And the role has changed quite a bit over the years.

One of our favorite quotes from Tina Fey's *Bossypants*—itself a fantastic primer for an improv-based leadership approach—is this: "There is not one management course in the world where they recommend self-righteousness as a tool."[34] Leadership today is all about letting go of the old stereotypes. If you have to demand respect, you never had it in the first place and you aren't going to get it through ultimatums.

Leadership today is a far cry from the cigar-chomping, throne-sitting, order-barking man in charge who dominated the cartoons of our childhood. The best contemporary leaders are skilled at operating in an ever-shifting dynamic that allows them to shift as well, letting the most knowledgeable staff members take center stage when necessary, and assuming more direct control of the environment when it's called for. Interestingly, studies show that these leadership traits are more commonly found in women than men.

Dr. Jack Zenger, along with Joseph Folkman, did a study in leadership in 2011 that sampled 7,280 leaders. And although males had a much higher percentage of the top leadership positions inside the organizations they analyzed, out of the fifteen functions of leadership effectiveness, females were rated more positively in twelve of them. Chief executive, author, and blogger Margaret Heffernan paraphrased Dr. Zenger's explanation for this finding in an article she wrote for *CBS MoneyWatch*:

> Women outscore men in leadership effectiveness . . . This is due primarily to a change in leadership styles. Moving from a command-and-control style of leadership to a more collaborative model plays . . . to women's strengths. Women are better listeners, better at building relationships, and more collaborative and that, he argues, makes them better adapted to the demands of modern leadership.[35]

Here are some of the areas in which women scored higher than men:

- Collaboration and Teamwork
- Inspires and Motivates Others
- Develops Others
- Champions Change
- Communicates Powerfully and Prolifically
- Practices Self-Development[36]

All of those qualities are found in the best improvisers. Does this make women overall better leaders than men? We know a number of people who would say just that. Not Betsy Myers, though. Myers is the former COO for Barack Obama's presidential campaign and a highly regarded leadership adviser who collaborated on several client engagements with Second City Works. She simply believes that we are now living in a time that necessitates a more balanced approach to leadership:

> The female approach to leadership is more about collaboration. It's more about listening and bringing people together and saying yes. Five years from now, the female workforce will be the majority. What worked yesterday isn't going to work tomorrow. Now, I'm not saying that the answer is to get rid of all the male qualities. We just need some balance. In the future, I think successful CEOs and leaders will follow the Yes, And philosophy. They won't be leading from the old command-and-control approach anymore. They'll lead from the worldview of "What do you think?" "You matter." "You're included." We're just using social tools that are historically more feminine.[37]

For us at The Second City, the prevalence of successful women in leadership roles is an endorsement of emotional intelligence and the so-called soft skills, which are precisely the kinds of abilities that improvisation serves to support, such as communicating, adapting to change, empathizing, and following instincts.

The ability of a leader to excel in those specific areas is more often than not in direct correlation with her effectiveness in leadership. If those qualities are the goal, improvisation is the practice in getting there. And all people, men and women alike, can use their soft skills more effectively if they have on-going and sustained practice using them as part of their everyday lives.

So here's a little leadership practice for you:

Who's the Leader?

In this exercise, the group forms a circle and one person stands in the center of the circle and closes her eyes. While the center person's eyes are closed, the rest of the group silently establishes which one of them is to be the leader. The group's job is to follow the leader's movements without speaking, slowly and deliberately. When the person in the middle opens her eyes, it is her job to figure out who the leader is. The game is over when the person in the middle identifies the leader.

What are we learning when we conduct this exercise? That in order to lead, we must be followed, and that requires clear and concise movements. The followers, for their part, must focus on the leader, paying attention to his or her movements as well as anticipating the next movement. The person in the middle also learns how quickly she is able to recognize leadership, or, if the scene in the exercise resembles anarchy, when leadership is not working. If the movement is fluid and precise, the leader should be easy to spot.

How does this look at your job? Is your boss transparent or

is leadership primarily an art of obfuscation? As an employee, are you focused on what your boss wants? Ideally, the point to remember is that leadership doesn't exist in a vacuum. There is a part to be played by all parties—by the leader and the led.

Silent Organization

In this exercise, your group will stand and line themselves up from youngest to oldest—without speaking. That doesn't mean they have to remain silent; they can communicate through any other means than language: noises, physical cues, or eye contact, for example. Repeat the exercise with a variety of other initiations, such as lining up in alphabetical order by last name or by their start date at the company; then try more difficult scenarios, like asking them to line up from most optimistic to pessimistic, or in alphabetical order of their favorite bands.

When we lose language, we are forced to find new ways to communicate. First and foremost, Silent Organization forces each individual to play a role in completing the task—it can't be done otherwise. Further, it requires a heightened focus on the other person—in some cases, inhabiting the moment to figure out what they are telling you with their movements, or in the case of the favorite band, seeing if you have information about that individual that might be pertinent to your business at hand, and using it. Doing the exercise—particularly with a team that has worked together for a while—can produce some interesting results. For some, the act is easy and intuitive; for others, it is much harder to grasp. Recognizing which team members have a natural ability to communicate and which don't should help everyone in the group.

Leadership practice doesn't all have to be silent. Here's a game with words:

String of Pearls

The group lines up face forward. The first person in line is given the first line of dialogue and the last person in line is given the last. Once the first line of dialogue is spoken, each succeeding member must improvise a line that will help logically move the story from its first line to its last. It might go something like this:

> First Line: One day, a cheetah delivered a pizza to my door.
> Last Line: I got a promotion at work.

Now it's the job of the three people between the first and the last to figure out how to move the narrative from the cheetah to the promotion. For them to come up with anything that makes sense, they will be required not only to look at how their part fits in the story, but also how the person's line before and after them fits in as well.

> Second Line: I was amazed, so I snapped a photo with my phone.
> Third Line: I sent that photo to my boss.
> Fourth Line: My boss is the photo editor of a wildlife magazine that was doing a feature on pizza.

More often than not, individuals are thrust into leadership roles with little to no training. So it isn't surprising at all that novice managers may assume a leadership style that sequesters knowledge and reinforces the separation between the leader and those being led. The unfortunate result of that style of leadership is that it becomes ingrained in both individuals and institutions, forming a barrier to innovation and growth.

Follow the Follower teaches us that there is a better way to lead. Managers don't need to control every aspect of their work-force in order to achieve the greatest results. In fact, the opposite is true. When managers can access and apply the best ideas and initiatives of the individuals they oversee, they gain a strategic advantage.

LISTENING IS A
MUSCLE

In 2004 British satirist Tony Hendra published a book called *Father Joe*. You may know Hendra from his role as Ian Faith, manager of the fictional band *Spinal Tap*. He was also an important contributor to *National Lampoon* and *Spy* magazine in the heydays of those two publications. His book, however, is a personal account of his decades-long friendship with a Benedictine monk named Father Joseph Warrilow.

As a young man, Hendra became involved with a married Catholic woman in his village in England. When the husband found out, Hendra was taken to the local priest to be "saved." Instead of giving Hendra the stick, Father Joe offered wise and compassionate counsel—something he continued to offer Hendra for decades, during regular respites from the comedian's rather reckless life.

In the early 1970s, Hendra began working with various Second City alumni such as John Belushi in the *Lampoon*'s production of *Lemmings*. He was astounded and confounded by their ability to perform off the top of their heads. He began to ask questions about improvisation. He writes in *Father Joe*:

> The advice I'd gotten from every source, if I wanted to arrive at a similar apotheosis, was listen. Listen at every level—to the words, the emotions, the intent of the other or others. Be completely open to them, bring nothing preconceived or prepared to the moment. Listen and then speak only to what you've heard. Do that, and you can't go wrong. Improv is not just a means to entertain, it's also a process that is an end in itself, a way of knowing, of grasping the nature of another, the reality of the other's existence, an aspect of the truth of the matter under discussion which you thought you knew but didn't until this moment.[38]

We were a bit startled to read such an impassioned and lovely account of improvisation by someone not strictly "of" the work, but it was the following passages in the book that caused it to be passed around our theatre for weeks on end, inspiring all sorts of discussion and argument:

> Hadn't Father Joe twenty or more years ago said an almost identical thing? The only way to know God, the only way to know the other, is to listen. Listening is reaching out into that unknown other self, surmounting your walls and theirs.[39]

Hendra quotes Father Joe as saying: "None of us listen enough, do we, dear? We only listen to a fraction of what people say. It's a wonderfully useful thing to do. You almost always hear something you didn't expect."[40]

Finally Hendra concludes: "No question that there were startling parallels between what the fathers of Improv and Father Joe had to say. Between Second City and the City of God."[41]

First, don't worry. We're not trying to start a religion. There are already too many self-identified gurus and masters, along with a sea of eager and well-meaning disciples who pray at the altar of various improv gods. But there is absolute truth here. To quote John Wayne, we're "short on ears and long on mouth." Anyone who is a parent or is in a relationship knows exactly what we're talking about.

According to *Forbes* columnist Glenn Lopis, 85 percent of what we know we learn through listening, and 45 percent of our workdays are spent listening, yet humans only listen at a 25 percent comprehension rate.[42] More alarming, Lopis finds that only 2 percent of professionals have actually taken any formal training in listening skills. It's hard to imagine such nonchalance about a foundational skill all of us need, and it's an oversight you'd never see in other fields. Can you imagine only 2 percent of professional baseball players taking batting practice? Try to contemplate only 2 percent of opera singers taking professional lessons and ongoing training. (Interesting side note: In both these fields, the cost of letting core skills go unpracticed is not only to lose out on work and opportunity, but also to look bad in public. Perhaps people only make the effort to improve themselves when they have to, when the cost of failure is concrete and visceral.)

We have a listening problem—in our world, in our country, at our places of business, in our homes. Why? Because we don't practice. Because we aren't taught. Sure, we're told to listen—by our parents, by our teachers—but despite the fact that listening is the primary means by which we learn, we've never been given the tools to develop our listening skills.

In our professional development classes, we make a real effort to show what business and improv have in common: We both have audiences to reach and win over, we both have to create and work on teams, and we both feel the pressure to perform, or be replaced by more talented and differently gifted performers. We also point out the important differences between our worlds. We find strength in ensembles over individuals, we're comfortable—or at least competent—in the absence of a script or plan, *and* we listen.

Great listening is at the core of great improvisation. As we've discovered, in order to build scenes onstage without a script to guide the action, actors need to affirm and build on each other's ideas—to use Yes, And—to create a cool, funny, smart scene. But before you can affirm and build on ideas, you must hear them in the first place. You must listen.

If someone starts a scene with, "I never knew scuba gear was so uncomfortable," and his scene partner responds with, "This city is getting overrun with Corgis," the scene goes nowhere. You know someone wasn't listening, and you'll have to strap in for what we sometimes call "badprov."

At The Second City, our actors go beyond mere *active* listening, which seeks to improve communication by having the listener rephrase what the speaker has said in order to assure that he or she understands the speaker's full intent. Active listening is the "Yes." To excel at improvisational listening, you still need to provide the "And." In improv, you understand that every word your scene partners utter is a gift, a lifeline, because it offers the rest of the ensemble something to build on, something from which they can make a scene funny and watchable. It's especially obvious who hasn't yet perfected his or her listening skills when you watch the beginning students' very first shows presented in our Training Center. Not surprisingly, the shows are laced with scenes that flail, actors who don't support each other, and ideas that never build. It's not because the students don't care or try; it's because they're still learning how to listen, and when the pressure is on, fear often overrides their listening skills. The students get so nervous they resort to all the fear-based responses we've talked about, such as yelling and questioning. The late, great cofounder of The Second City Training Center, Martin de Maat, observed that nervous young students often resort to falling into "story." They will simply keep talking about something, anything, in a nonstop monologue, unconnected to the people working or events happening around them onstage. Basically, they are talking rather than listening.

Do you know anyone like that at your job?

In improvisation, we often talk in terms of gifts and offerings. When other actors say something, that's a gift to you and the scene, and if everyone is listening fully, building on what's being offered, great scenes are possible. The same thing holds in a work environment. If you're doing all the talking, you're not really listening to what others are offering, and your exchanges with coworkers are less productive than they could be. To underscore the importance of this idea, we often include the improv exercise Thank You in our work with corporate clients. In this exercise, people pair up and have conversations about anything at all, but before one can respond to a partner's thoughts, he or she has to say "thank you" for what the other person offered. It's a little stilted, of course, but it really helps underscore the value we should be attaching to the ideas of others in everyday conversation. Thank You helps us remember that as important as our own words and ideas are, those of the people around us are just as important and valuable.

To counter the natural impulse not to hear or value others' ideas, one of the very early exercises we teach in our classes is Repetition, in which students must repeat or paraphrase the dialogue they just heard from their scene partner before providing their own new dialogue. That's active listening—Listening 101. As students advance through the classes, with any luck, they will learn and practice enough of this active listening that they will fully hear their scene partner's words, rather than plan what they are going to say next.

Have you ever witnessed or, God forbid, been the speaker in the room who lost his train of thought? As you became more and more self-conscious, your throat probably went dry, you started to perspire, and suddenly all your knowledge and preparation went out the window. That's because self-consciousness smothers our ability to communicate effectively. But an individual who is steeped in the practice of listening can keep the demons of self-doubt at bay when this happens. It allows them to focus on the ideas and other people in the room, not on themselves. That's why Elliott Masie didn't panic when he found himself in the middle of a real-life actor's nightmare—being expected to speak in front of a crowd on a topic he knew nothing about, as described in Chapter Seven. He just listened, and in doing so, he gave his audience exactly what they wanted.

Deep, practiced listening is really a form of meditation. It is a skill that enables you to turn off the judgment part of your brain and allows you to interact with individuals and groups in a seamless way. It is not too much to say that great listening is the difference between flopping in front of 300 people and creating art.

When we're improvising onstage, we're not just listening to scene partners, we're listening to audience suggestions. And sometimes we're listening to mistakes, so that we can abide by yet another improv adage, "Make mistakes work for you."

We've seen it play itself out night after night on our stages, and the results are always the same. The mistake is often as simple as not getting a name right. For example, a scene begins,

Actor A has been given the name Paul, and Actor B has been given the name Steve. Later in the scene, Actor A refers to Actor B as Bill. The audience knows that a mistake has been made. The other actors onstage know a mistake has been made. Everyone knows a mistake has been made except for Actor A.

In this mistake, Actor B sees an opportunity.

Rather than call out the mistake—which wouldn't be funny and would take everyone out of the scene—the actor who has been listening deeply and is engaged in the moment will take the mistake and weave it into the narrative. And so Actor B replies,

"So when did you find out my real identity?"

The crowd goes wild. They recognize that a transformation has just happened onstage, turning a potentially embarrassing moment into something cool and funny.

Maybe it's to be expected that improvisers listen better than the average person, since failing to do so results in public, humiliating failure onstage. When we don't listen, we bore the shit out of the audience, and we suffer the consequences immediately. Also, bad listeners are not great scene partners, and if word gets around improv circles, nobody's going to want to play with them onstage. So with the stakes that high, our improvisers learn to listen or die.

Offstage in the business world, or anywhere people communicate, we don't always feel the consequences of poor listening immediately. When you're drifting off during a boss's rant or listening with one ear to your spouse recounting the challenges of the day, you may miss some opportunities to connect, but you're also likely to get away with it, because you can often hide exactly how checked out you are. Nod a few times, murmur a few um-hums, and a lot of people will mistake these superficial expressions of listening as the real deal.

But just because people can get away being bad listeners doesn't mean that there is no cost.

So what is the cost to bad listening? You build things no one asked for and no one wanted.

In our business, we have seen this in action when we hire a director to put together a sketch comedy show, and when we see the first preview, the show onstage is not a sketch comedy show. The director has decided to "innovate" and create a play or a musical or some other theatrical conceit that in its present state won't work for the intended audience. Senior management has been guilty of this as well. A bunch of Second City producers—we're not naming names, Kelly—decided that the world needed to see a live theatrical adaptation of the iconic hockey film *Slapshot*. Turns out, you can't keep an audience from not coming to your show. Was anyone asking to see live theatrical versions of *Lord of the Rings*, *Carrie*, or *Spiderman*? They weren't, and those shows lost millions and millions of dollars before closing. As content creators, we need to listen to each other in order to build something new. As theatre producers, we need to listen to our audiences to make sure that they want the new thing we are building. In business, there are thousands if not millions of examples of products that no one ever wanted, and if the producers had just listened to their audience, they would not have wasted so much money making the thing in the first place.

- Ben-Gay aspirin
- Cosmopolitan yogurt
- McDonald's Arch Deluxe
- Harley Davidson perfume
- The XFL
- New Coke

You could say that all these ideas were off-brand, but off-brand is what happens when a company doesn't listen to its own client base. Were Coke drinkers actively telling the company that they no longer enjoyed the taste of Coke? How could Mc-Donald's believe that their customers were looking for a more "sophisticated" item on their menu? And the idea of Ben-Gay aspirin is just really, really gross.

THE PRACTICE OF LISTENING

You could make the case that listening skills are more important than ever, given the macro changes happening in the world. As business becomes more global and generational shifts occur in earnest in the workplace, it's more important than ever to improve the quality of communications, not just the volume of it. And in order to improve the quality of communications, people need to improve their listening skills; you can't have one without the other. Much to our delight, and to that of our clients, we've found that people really can become better listeners and communicators with committed practice. Listening is like a muscle—it needs to be worked in order to see improvement. And we've created a battery of exercises that make improvement not only possible, but also fun to do.

One example of a great listening skills exercise is Last Word Response. In this exercise, we pair people up and instruct them to have a conversation about anything at all, business-related or not. The only catch is that participants must begin whatever they say with the last word spoken by their partner. In practice, it might sound something like this:

PERSON 1 Boy, I love hot summer days. Can't wait to go for a run and jump into the pool after work.
PERSON 2 Work has been hard lately. I'm really struggling to connect with my new boss.

PERSON 1   Boss is a title I've never liked much. I like to collaborate more than to give orders.
PERSON 2   Orders get clogged up all the time in our procurement system.

You get the idea. It's not important that the conversation actually make any sense. In fact, it's more fun if it doesn't. But an exercise like Last Word Response is a great way to demonstrate how poorly we tend to listen to colleagues in everyday conversation—because in order to be successful, the participants *must listen to each other all the way through* to the end of a thought. They can't check out halfway through the other person's statement and do the exercise right. Listening through to the end of a speaker's thought is not something many of us are used to doing, either in business or in life. More often, we check out partway through or get busy formulating a response or counterpoint before they even finish speaking. In his book *The 7 Habits of Highly Effective People*, Stephen R. Covey called this the difference between "listening to understand and listening to respond."[43] In any event, by not listening all the way through, two unfortunate things can happen. First, we might miss the actual content of what someone says because we've disengaged, so our response may be innocuously irrelevant. Worse, we may say something that directly contradicts the first speaker's statement simply because we didn't listen to the end. We can find ourselves in disagreement when we don't really disagree at all, because we didn't take the time to listen to everything that was being said before we opened our mouth. Those lessons learned through improv have allowed political adviser Betsy Myers to retain her optimism, even though today's political climate could have made her the worst kind of cynic. She insists that "if you listen, if you truly listen, you'll realize how easy it is to connect with people you thought you disagreed with. That's the freedom you get with improv."[44]

After doing literally thousands of workshops for corporate clients, we can say definitively that businesspeople are wired to be responders, not generous, empathetic listeners. Some of this certainly stems from the unconscious desire to control the direction of a conversation, which seems to be a conditioned response in business. But it's interesting how counterproductive this habit can actually be, especially if control is the goal. In our experience, it's the generous communicators and empathetic listeners who ultimately earn the highest status in the room. They come across as more self-assured because they have confidence that, no matter what they hear, they will be able to come up with an appropriate and useful response. Most businesspeople, however, are so caught up in giving the "right" response that they miss the essence of the conversation that's unfolding. And if you get two or more of those folks in a meeting, they both look smaller and less influential with each attempt to jockey for the upper hand by talking past each other.

Last Word Response not only teaches us to listen more fully, it also shows us how generous and "other-directed" we can be. People who regularly frame their comments as questions or end their statements in prepositions make it very hard for their partners to respond easily in this exercise. For example:

PERSON 1   I pushed my idea pretty hard, but I wasn't sure where he was at.

Or

PERSON 1   How about you?

In either case, it's possible to respond starting with the last word, but it's usually a struggle. Some people who desire to be in control of a conversation do this on purpose, but it's just as common in individuals who are simply not paying attention—either to their partner or to their own words. We find that generous communicators and listeners are attentive to this and will do their best to set their partners up for an easier response. Their goal isn't to stump their partner; it's to set him up for success.

LISTENING FOR INTENT

Improvisation is a highly verbal medium, but words are only one way in which we communicate. Often, words aren't enough to convey a speaker's true intent. The tone or manner in which we speak provides a host of meanings for listeners to discern. Additionally, the physical cues that we use during a conversation provide another layer of communication. Paul Ekman codeveloped the concept of micro expressions, extremely brief facial expressions that appear when people conceal their true emotions, deliberately or unconsciously. Ekman's group identified seven universal micro expressions: anger, fear, sadness, disgust, contempt, surprise, and happiness. Learning to spot them is tough—they appear for only a fraction of a second—but good face readers can learn a lot about how vast the gulf can be between what we say and how we really feel. And getting to the subtext of what someone is saying is a basic trope of comedy. It's where a lot of the laughter comes from.

In the 2000 revue *Better Late Than Nader*, Andy Cobb and Debra Downing performed a scene called "Talk Like Lovers," in which the characters' dialogue was the actual subtext of what they were saying:

ANDY   Idle banter.

DEB   Chatter, chatter, chatter.

ANDY   Reference to mutually shared inside joke.

DEB   Polite laughter. Offhand remark.

ANDY   Sports reference.

DEB   No idea.

ANDY   Inappropriate double entendre.

BOTH   Awkward silence.

ANDY   Mustering of confidence. Statement of evening's purpose.

BOTH   Eye contact, eye contact, eye contact.

ANDY   Compliment of appearance.

DEB   Coy denial.

It is absolutely vital for improvisers to key in on what's *really* being said in addition to what *is* being said. So much comedy springs from that source, such as Abbott and Costello's famous "Who's on first?" routine, or almost any of the scenarios improvised by Nichols and May. Beyond comedic purposes, empathetic listening gives you a far clearer path to truth. When you understand how someone is feeling in addition to what they are saying, you receive multiple insights into their whole psyche. This widens the possibilities of communication. It is the same thing as what Ekman refers to as cognitive empathy, which Dan Goleman, author of *Emotional Intelligence*, explains as "simply knowing how the other person feels and what they might be thinking. Sometimes called perspective-taking, this kind of empathy can help in, say, a negotiation or in motivating people."[45]

We take our corporate clients through a variety of exercises to teach them the importance of getting beyond words as a way to improve internal and external communication, to move faster to "yes" when trying to sell to a client, and to make such interchange a key player in research and development.

Representatives from an advertising company approached us for help with their account executives and creative director. They weren't interested in just improving the team's abilities to land clients, but also in keeping the clients they had. They observed that their team had lost business by misreading their now former clients' signals. Sometimes unhappy clients are not going to tell you directly that they are unhappy. Better to find that out before they take their business elsewhere.

We took account executives Jen and Tim and creative director Nate through a sequence called "Touch to Talk and Eye Contact to Speak." They weren't allowed to talk unless they made physical or strong eye contact with their partner. Over a few minutes, this simple exercise required Jen, Tim, and Nate to form a specific physical connection to each other before they could communicate. When repeated, this practice instills a foundational need to fully pay attention to others. At the same time, individuals experience how powerful it feels when others pay full attention to us.

We followed that with a Gibberish Game. Jen and Tim both spoke in complete gibberish—made-up words and sounds—while Nate was tasked with "translating" what they said to the others in the room. At first, Nate tried to make jokes about the gibberish. We let him. But after that first round—in which Nate did get a lot of laughs—we asked him to try it again. But this time, his job wasn't to make jokes. We wanted Nate to really *listen* to the gibberish. We forced him to pay closer attention not only to the silly sounds he heard, but to the body language of Tim and Jen, who were likewise asked to try to communicate something with their gibberish.

The whole mood of the room changed. Nate focused intently

on Jen and Tim as he started to describe what they were expressing. Jen's voice was trembling and she was shivering. "I'm cold, I need a jacket, or you need to turn up the heat," Nate translated—to which Jen smiled, as he had gotten it exactly right. Tim's portrayal was harder to get. He held his head high, puffed out his chest, and assumed an air of grandness. Finally, Nate struck gold when he translated, "I'm the boss. I'm in charge. Someone get me a coffee!" The room erupted in laughter, as the other employees recognized that Tim had been portraying the president of their company, demonstrating that Nate was able to hear through the gibberish.

By repeating these exercises and absorbing the experience of listening for intent, the advertising group learned to focus on more than their clients' words in order to gauge how effectively their relationships were being managed. Clients want to be heard, they just don't always use the most direct language to express themselves. With this new understanding, the team was able to improve their client retention rate, as well as increase the ease with which they landed new clients.

Ekman writes, "Improving your ability to recognize others' emotions will increase the intimacy and understanding with which you connect with other people. Research has also found that people who learn to spot micro expressions were better liked by coworkers."[46]

His theories dovetail nicely with the core elements of improvisation. It should come as no surprise that Ekman was at the University of Chicago with Mike Nichols and Elaine May in the early 1950s—at the same time that they were practicing the improvisational theatre games of Viola Spolin with her son Paul, the original artistic director of The Second City.

"Improvisational listeners" are more effective listeners because they go into every conversation looking to build on what the other person offers. This isn't to suggest that improvisational listeners are soft or lack the ability to forcefully advocate their position. It just means that they understand that their advocacy is grounded in and improved by what is actually being said by others. It doesn't exist in an echo chamber.

Sales calls, creative meetings where different visions are being expressed, and one-on-one employee reviews are essential moments of communication; how well you listen at these crucial times can determine the success or failure of your entire business. If you are not practicing total listening, you are not bringing your A-game to the endeavor, which, practically speaking, doesn't make any sense if you want to succeed.

One of the most successful videos in our RealBiz Shorts series lampooned a typical conference call. It was a comic ballet in not listening. One caller is driving and keeps cutting in and out as you hear the horns and wails of street traffic; another's reception is so bad she sounds like the teacher in the *Peanuts* cartoons talking through a haze of static; someone else keeps interrupting because he's not even sure why he's on the call in the first place. Funny because it's true, right?

We often talk about which tenet of improvisation is the most important. Usually it's different for each person, and it's different in each situation. But it just might be that we could change the world if enough people used improv to become better listeners. If more people listened with empathy, there would be fewer misunderstandings, leading to less conflict; if listening were highlighted throughout our education, we would help create individuals who instinctively cared what other people felt and thought. Just imagine the possibilities inherent in large groups of people actively, purposefully, professionally listening to one another. That's a world we want to live in.

CONCLUSION:

WHAT HAPPENED WHEN WE
YES, ANDED THE WRITING OF
THIS BOOK

> You use it at work, you use it at home. I know there are
> commercial reasons to do improv. But for me, the main
> argument for improv is that it makes your life better
> and richer and more interesting.
> —Michael Lewis, author of *Moneyball* and *Flash Boys*[47]

Ultimately, improvisation is about making discoveries. You walk
onto the stage or into a room with absolutely nothing and, by
the time you leave, you will have created something. The quality
of that something depends on a variety of factors, almost all of
which come down to how well you and your team can apply your
brains and your heart to the task at hand.

At The Second City, we have had the privilege of observing

and documenting the act of creativity for more than half a century. On the stage and in the classroom, we have tested our principles and applied our techniques in literally millions of scenarios. And what we have learned is that there is no one definitive path, no one way, no line from point A to point B that will make you excel at your work, or be more creative and collaborative, or a better communicator. But we can give you tools that will aid you in whatever path you end up taking.

The writing of this book has been an act of improvisation, and we have made countless discoveries along the way. As we studied improvisation's role in developing leaders, we came across Malcolm Knowles's eight tenets of leadership. We were particularly intrigued by the fourth: "The creative leader highly values individuality. The sense that people operate on a higher level when they are operating on the basis of their unique strengths, interests, talents, and goals than when they are trying to conform to some imposed stereotype and tightly defined set of assigned responsibilities."[48] That idea sparked a memory. As we write this conclusion, we are mourning the death of Second City alum Harold Ramis. The prolific actor/writer/director whose credits include *Animal House, Ghostbusters, Stripes, Caddyshack*, and *Groundhog Day*, to name only a few, was a beloved mentor at our theatre. While looking through tapes of Harold speaking on various panels throughout the years, we found this passage from December 1999:

"Most people think of directing as a control function. Really, at Second City, it's more of a facilitative function, at the risk of making up a word—being a facilitator and helping people recognize their best work, as opposed to telling them how to do it or how you see the show. Traditionally, we think the director takes a piece of material, interprets it, and then finds actors to fulfill his vision of it. That's not Second City. You have people who are constantly firing new ideas out. You help them catch the best ones and shape them and maybe see connections that they don't see, and then give it a kind of polish."

Knowles and Ramis were talking about the same thing: Leadership is about building strong ensembles in which individuals participate by virtue of their strengths, and are supported despite their weaknesses.

If we wish to thrive in the innovation sphere, we are going to have to destigmatize failure. The founders of this theatre understood that in 1959, and they paved the way to create one of the most successful theatres in the country's history—a theatre whose core business, it should be noted, is original work.

Throughout the writing process, we spent hours upon hours in each other's offices, asking ourselves if we were getting it right. We certainly hope we did, but those conversations revealed to us another important truth:

We can't be held inert by the fear of not being right. We get it wrong—a lot of the time. We forget the tenets of improvisation and we shut people down, stop listening, and say "No, But" rather than "Yes, And."

But here's the important part: We reflect on those lapses in judgment. We say we're sorry. And we work to do better.

This revolution we are experiencing has no room for absolutes. The world is shifting, accelerating, and demanding more of us. Keeping up can be a challenge, whether you're trying to ride the waves of change and innovation, or make the waves yourself. Regardless, there's no need to be afraid—improvisation is the perfect tool kit for navigating the unknown.

ONE LAST LIST

We may have cool jobs, but they are jobs, nonetheless. Over the course of time, we have seen jobs done well and jobs done badly. A few years ago we created a list that we taped to the wall in our office. We leave you with these words of advice, born of an improvisational theatre, but applicable, we think, to everyone, everywhere, who wants to be better at what they do.

> Look people in the eye when you meet them.
> Smile.
> Don't check your texts or e-mail when someone else is talking.
> Be curious.
> Try to eliminate the word *no* from your vocabulary for just one day.
> When you are wrong, acknowledge it, say you're sorry, and move on.
> Forgive yourself and forgive others.
> Lead as you would want to be led.
> Don't be an asshole, and don't abide assholes.
> Be on time.
> Excel at preparation.
> Ask yourself, what is the problem you are trying to solve?
> Make your partner look good.
> Respect, don't revere.
> Listen to the whole person.
> Read the room.
> Share the conversation.
> Love your work.
> Applaud others.

Say *we* rather than *I* whenever possible.

Consider that you might not be right.

Open your door.

Try not to work out of fear; work from a sense of
   possibility.

Understand the audience you're trying to win over, and
   give them a role.

Be an improviser.

APPENDIX:

THE SECOND CITY IMPROV EXERCISES

Throughout this book we've offered a number of exercises for you to try within your own organizations. They make a lot to remember, however, so we've listed them all here for easy reference, along with reminders about what purpose they can serve.

1. EXERCISE: EXPOSURE, 22

SETUP: Divide your group into two lines, facing each other, about ten feet apart. Have the two groups stand looking at each other. Give this some time, and once there is noticeable discomfort, have them look somewhere else in the room, to complete a counting task (e.g., bricks on the wall, ceiling tiles, etc.). The fidgeting and discomfort will stop, with everyone instead concentrating on the task at hand.

POINT OF FOCUS: To have participants discover that focus can help rid them of fear and being in their heads.

2. EXERCISE: WORD AT A TIME STORY, 42

SETUP: Gather six to ten people in a circle, and ask them to tell an original story, each contributing one word at a time. The first participant commences with a single word, the action moving in one direction around the circle. Each successive player contributes one word toward the overall narrative. The exercise plays out over several minutes, and a story develops that takes hilarious and unexpected twists and turns.

POINT OF FOCUS: Yes, Anding: Individual participants affirm and build in their unique way to a far more interesting story than they would probably have come up with on their own.

3. EXERCISE: TALK WITHOUT I, 58

SETUP: Pair participants up and instruct them to have a conversation about anything at all—without using the word *I*. After running the exercise, talk about what it took to be successful to complete it and how it might help participants when sharing ideas or evaluating the recommendations of others.

POINT OF FOCUS: Ensemble: It helps focus on speaking without *I* and it demands that one speaker be aware of the other.

4. EXERCISE: MIRROR, 70

SETUP: Split participants up into pairs facing each other. Assign one person the job to lead by making small movements with her face and body; the other person is to mirror every action of the first. Then have the pair switch leaders. Finally, see if they can mirror each other when no one is assigned to lead.

POINT OF FOCUS: Building ensemble: The exercise gives people a chance to know what it feels like to tap into all their powers of observation and focus with a partner.

5. EXERCISE: GIVE AND TAKE, 71

SETUP: Have your group spread out in the room. Starting with one person, ask them to "give focus" to another team member, using a simple physical cue (e.g., looking them in the eye, pointing at them, or touching them on the shoulder). Next, ask the group to "take focus" in the same manner (e.g., by standing in front of them or waving their arms while standing next to them). Finally, challenge the group to do it all—give focus, then take focus, then give it back.

POINT OF FOCUS: Ensemble work: Ideally, the various team members will become adept at giving and taking focus in equal measure, which can help make brainstorming sessions more fruitful and loosen up strategy meetings.

6. EXERCISE: PARTS OF A WHOLE, 80

SETUP: With the group spread out in the room, suggest some item that they can organize themselves into (e.g., an animal, a truck, a printer). Have the participants use their bodies to create that shape, each individual forming a different part. Next, suggest something slightly more complex (e.g., shoppers in a grocery store, fish in an aquarium, etc.).

POINT OF FOCUS: Ensemble work: The exercise stresses the point that individuals seeking to succeed while working in a group must be willing to cede control and play their part.

7. EXERCISE: TAKE THAT BACK, 133

SETUP: Players improvise a scene based on a suggestion. Each time the leader rings a bell the actor speaking must replace his last sentence, phrase, or word with a different one and continue the scene from there.

For example:

PLAYER   I have a dog.

DING!

PLAYER   I have a cat.

DING!

PLAYER   I have a rash.

And the scene continues . . .

POINT OF FOCUS: To focus on the here and now: To get the players out of their heads and to be able not to preplan or think about their next offer.

VARIATIONS: Can be played without a bell, the instructor simply calling out "Take that back!" or "New choice!" In this variation, the leader may occasionally ask a player to replace an action rather than a phrase, for example: "Take back that accent!" or "New dance move!"

8. EXERCISE: THANK YOU STATUES, 136

SETUP: Have the group form a large circle. Ask for a volunteer to go first. Have the individual step into the middle of the circle and strike a pose, any pose. Once he is set, another participant will step into the middle, tap the first person out, and assume her own pose. The first person will say "thank you" and take his place back in the circle. After a couple rounds of this, the group picks up the tempo so that things move more quickly. Eventually, they stop tapping out the person posing in the center, and just go one-by-one to the middle and take a pose that builds on those of the others already there, ultimately creating a statue. When only two people are left in the circle, ask them to name the statue that has been created.

POINT OF FOCUS: Co-Creation: The exercise helps participants enhance their ability to put ideas out there without fear of judgment by peers or coworkers. Instead, the focus is on supporting one another's ideas and not getting caught up in their own.

9. EXERCISE: EMOTIONAL OPTION, OR EMO OP, 138

SETUP: Divide the group into pairs. Have the pairs start a conversation about anything at all. As they talk, begin to shout out different emotions at various points. Once an emotion is cued, the pairs must continue the conversation in the tone of that emotion.

POINT OF FOCUS: Co-Creation: It teaches how to better deal with change and how to communicate more effectively with your peers.

10. EXERCISE: FOLLOW THE FOLLOWER, 167

SETUP: Have group members sit in a circle. On the leader's cue, everyone in the circle should start to make sounds and movements. However, at the same time, they must also mimic *the sounds and movements of the others* in the circle.

POINT OF FOCUS: Ensemble leadership: This is practice for focusing attention on the others in the group so that ultimately, they learn to work together as one unit.

11. EXERCISE: WHO'S THE LEADER? 189

SETUP: Have the group stand in a circle, with one member in the middle—eyes closed. The rest of the group then silently chooses one member to be the leader, whose body language and movements they slowly and silently begin to mimic. When called to do so, the member in the middle opens her eyes and tries to figure out who in the circle is the leader.

POINT OF FOCUS: Leadership and observation: This helps individuals understand that leadership works in a dynamic that is always changing.

12. EXERCISE: SILENT ORGANIZATION, 190

SETUP: Have the group line up according to age, oldest to youngest. To do this, the players are allowed to communicate, as long as they don't use words—they can use only eye contact, noises, gestures, etc. Have them repeat the exercise, organizing members by increasingly abstract characteristics (most pessimistic to sunniest outlook; fewest siblings to most numerous, etc.).

POINT OF FOCUS: Leadership: This helps teach deeper and more effective communication and observation, especially relating to organizing a group of people to complete a task.

13. EXERCISE: STRING OF PEARLS, 191

SETUP: Have the group stand in a line facing forward. The person at one end of the line is given the first sentence of a story, and the person at the other end, the last sentence. The first person speaks the given opener, and then, going down the line, each participant improvises a succeeding line of dialogue until the last, who says the line he was given—the point being to make the progression from first to last as logical as possible.

POINT OF FOCUS: Listening: This is an excellent exercise to help people listen more closely and think harder about what others are saying before speaking themselves.

14. EXERCISE: REPETITION, 197

SETUP: Break your group into pairs. Have each pair sit or stand, facing each other. Have the two begin a conversation, each speaking one sentence at a time. The first person initiates with any random line of dialogue, but before her partner can answer, he must repeat the line she just said. This continues throughout the exercise.

For example:

PERSON 1 This new boss really knows how to dress.
PERSON 2 This new boss really knows how to dress. She's putting my pajama jeans to shame.

POINT OF FOCUS: Listening: This is practice in listening all the way through to the end of a speaker's thought before starting to form or express a response.

15. EXERCISE: LAST WORD RESPONSE, 201
. . . . .

SETUP: Divide your group into pairs. Just as in Repetition, have the pairs begin a conversation about anything at all, speaking one line at a time. However, instead of repeating the entire preceding sentence, they must start with *just the last word* of their partner's sentence.

For example:

PERSON 1   No matter what I do, I always fail my math tests.
PERSON 2   Tests—I've never been good at them.

POINT OF FOCUS: Listening: An exercise like Last Word Response is a great way to demonstrate how poorly we tend to listen to colleagues in everyday conversation.

16. EXERCISE: TOUCH TO TALK AND EYE CONTACT TO SPEAK, 206
. . . .

SETUP: With your group divided into pairs, have two members start a conversation. Neither individual can speak without first making physical or strong eye contact with the other.

POINT OF FOCUS: Listening: This exercise shows that people need a partner in order to talk. It's a way of setting a foundation for real communication.

17. EXERCISE: GIBBERISH GAMES, 206

SETUP: Select three group members. Two of them will have a conversation entirely in made-up words and sounds—gibberish. The third person "translates" the exchange for the rest of the group. Rotate parts and repeat.

POINT OF FOCUS: Listening and paying attention: The participants learn to focus on the whole person rather than the words alone in the course of communicating.

NOTES

1. Thomas L. Friedman, "How to Get a Job at Google," *New York Times*, February 22, 2014, www.nytimes.com/2014/02/23/opinion/sunday/friedman-how-to-get-a-job-at-google.html?_r=0 accessed.

2. Elliott Masie, CEO and founder of the MASIE Center, interviewed by the author, summer 2013. Interview recieved 8/12/13.

3. Dr. Mark Pfeffer, psychotherapist and director of the Panic/Anxiety Recovery Center in Chicago, interviewed by the author, summer 2013. Interview recieved 8/12/13.

4. Dr. Hal M. Lewis, president and CEO of the Spertus Institute for Jewish Learning and Leadership, interviewed by the author, summer 2013. Interview recieved 8/7/13.

5. "Growth Company Executives Want More Government Help to Drive Corporate Innovation, According to Ernst & Young Survey," Banking & Financial Services | Surveys, Polls and Research, PR Newswire, September 19, 2013, http://www.prnewswire.com/news-releases/growth-company-executives-want-more-government-help-to-drive-corporate-innovation-according-to-ernst—young-survey-78678432.html. Comment: Unable to access webpage.

6. "Linux," *Wikipedia, The Free Encyclopedia*, September 17, 2013, http://en.wikipedia.org/wiki/Linux.

7.   From Dictionary.com: dictionary.reference.com/browse/ensemble
           and dictionary.reference.com/browse/team.

8.   F. Scott Fitzgerald, "The Crack-Up," *Esquire*, February 1936.

9.   Phil Jackson and Michael Arkush, *The Last Season: A Team in Search
           of Its Soul* (New York: Penguin Books, 2005), 149.

10.   Adam Bryant, "Ensemble Acting, in Business," *New York Times*, June
           7, 2009, BU2.

11.   Joel H. Cohen, "He Loves to Fly and He D'ohs," (directed by Mark
           Kirkland), *The Simpsons*, Fox: September 23, 2007.

12.   Jeffrey Passel and D'Vera Cohn, "U.S. Population Projections:
           2005–2050," *Social and Demographic Trends* (2008): *Pew Research
           Center*, February 11, 2008, www.pewsocialtrends.org/2008/02/11/
           us-population-projections-2005-2050/.

13.   Adam Grant, *Give and Take: A Revolutionary Approach to Success* (New
           York: Penguin Group, 2013), 6.

14.   Sigmund Freud, *Civilization and Its Discontents* (London: Hogarth
           Press, 1930), 102–103.

15.   Sue Shellenbarger, "When the Boss Is a Screamer," *Wall Street Jour-
           nal*, August 15, 2012, online.wsj.com/news/articles/SB1000087239
           6390444772404577589302193682244.

16.   E. B. White and K. S. White, *A Subtreasury of American Humor* (New
           York: Coward-McCann, 1941), 402.

17.   Mel Brooks, director, *The 2,000-Year-Old Man*, Crossbow Produc-
           tions, Acre Enterprises, Leo Salkin Films, 1975.

18.   From Dictionary.com: dictionary.reference.com/browse/revere?s=t.

19.   Jason Fried, "Want to Know What Your Employees Really Think?,"
           Inc. magazine, October 2011, http://www.inc.com/magazine/201110/
           jason-fried-on-learning-what-your-employees-think.html.

20.   "Groupon founder Andrew Mason's farewell letter to employees,"
           Technology Blog, *Guardian*, March 1, 2013, www.theguardian.com/
           technology/blog/2013/mar/01/groupon-andrew-mason-fired-letter.

21.   Jason Fried, "Want to Know What Your Employees Really Think?,"
           Inc. magazine, October 2011, http://www.inc.com/magazine/201110/
           jason-fried-on-learning-what-your-employees-think.html.

22.   Lindsay Prossnitz, "*The Second City Guide to the Opera*," *Chicago
           Tonight*, January 3, 2013, chicagotonight.wttw.com/2013/01/03/
           second-city-guide-opera.

23.   John von Rhein, "Lyric, Second City Lovingly Skewer Opera," *Chicago*

Tribune, January 6, 2013, articles.chicagotribune.com/2013-01-06/ entertainment/ct-ent-0107-lyric-second-city-review-20130106_1_ lyric-opera-second-city-guide-ryan-opera-center/2.

24. David Ogilvy, *Ogilvy on Advertising* (New York City: Vintage Books, 1985, c 1983), 20.

25. Dick Costolo, "How to Run Your Company Like an Improv Group," *Bloomberg Businessweek,* April 11, 2013, www.businessweek.com/ articles/2013-04-11/how-to-run-your-company-like-an-improv-group-by-twitter-ceo-dick-costolo.

26. Jeremy Jackson, "Wanna Create a Great Product? Fail Early, Fail Fast, Fail Often," Co.Design, June 1, 2011, www.fastcodesign.com/1663968/ wanna-create-a-great-product-fail-early-fail-fast-fail-often.

27. Matthew Robinson, "The Culinary Arts: A Model for Innovation in Business," *Young Upstarts,* November 12, 2013, www.youngupstarts .com/2013/11/12/the-culinary-arts-a-model-for-innovation-in-business/.

28. Richard Langworth, *Churchill by Himself* (New York: PublicAffairs, 2011), 579.

29. P. F. Drucker, *Management: Tasks, Responsibilities, Practices* (New York: Harper & Row, 1974), 463.

30. P. F. Drucker, *Managing the Nonprofit Organization: Principles and Practices* (New York: HarperCollins, 1990), 18–19.

31. Elliott Masie, CEO and founder of the MAISIE Center, interviewed by the author, summer 2013. Interview received 8/12/13.

32. Anne Libera, *The Second City Almanac of Improvisation* (Chicago: Northwestern University Press, 2004), 56.

33. Dick Costolo, "How to Run Your Company Like an Improv Group," *Bloomberg Businessweek,* April 11, 2013, www.businessweek.com/ articles/2013-04-11/how-to-run-your-company-like-an-improv-group-by-twitter-ceo-dick-costolo.

34. Tina Fey, *Bossypants* (New York: Reagan Arthur/Little, Brown and Company, 2011), 128.

35. Margaret Heffernan, *MoneyWatch,* March 26, 2013, www.cbsnews .com/news/yes-women-make-better-leaders/.

36. Joseph Folkman and Jack Zenger, *A Study in Leadership: Women Do It Better Than Men,* Zenger/Folkman, March 30, 2012, zfco.com/ media/articles/ZFCo.WP.WomenBetterThanMen.033012.pdf.

37. Betsy Myers, interviewed by the author, summer 2013. Interview received 9/28/13.

38. Tony Hendra, *Father Joe* (New York: Random House, 2005), 181.

39. Ibid., 182.

40. Ibid.

41. Ibid.

42. Glenn Lopis, "6 Ways Effective Listening Can Make You a Better Leader," *Forbes*, May 20, 2013, www.forbes.com/sites/ glennllopis/2013/05/20/6-effective-ways-listening-can-make-you-a-better-leader/.

43. Stephen R. Covey, *The 7 Habits of Highly Effective People: Restoring the Character Ethic* (New York: Free Press, 2004), 258.

44. Betsy Myers, interviewed by the author, summer 2013. Interview received 9/28/13.

45. Daniel Goleman, "Three Kinds of Empathy: Cognitive, Emotional, Compassionate," DanielGoleman.info, June 7, 2007, http://www .danielgoleman.info/three-kinds-of-empathy-cognitive-emotional-compassionate/.

46. Paul Ekman Group, LLC, "Micro Expressions" (n.d.). Retrieved April 29, 2014, from http://www.paulekman.com/micro-expressions/.

47. Michael Lewis, author of *Moneyball* and *Flash Boys*, interviewed by the author, summer 2013. Interview received 9/27/13.

48. John M. McCann, "Leadership as Creativity: Finding the Opportunity Hidden Within Decision Making and Dialogue," Partners in Performance, Inc., 2012, http://www.partnersinperformance.us/ index.php?option=com_content&view=article&id=71&Itemid=62.

INDEX

ABOUT THE AUTHORS

Kelly Leonard is the executive vice president of The Second City and the president of Second City Theatricals. He has worked at The Second City since 1988 and has overseen productions with such notable performers as Stephen Colbert, Tina Fey, and Amy Poehler. Kelly cofounded Second City Theatricals, the division of the company that develops an eclectic array of live entertainment all over the world. He has fostered creative and business collaborations with Lyric Opera Chicago, Norwegian Cruise Line, Hubbard Street Dance, and the *Chicago Tribune*, to name a few.

Tom Yorton has been CEO of Second City Works, the b2b arm of The Second City, since 2002. Before joining The Second City family, Tom worked in advertising and marketing at agencies like Ogilvy, Grey, and Hal Riney before jumping to the client side, with stints as a marketing vice president at Sears and 3Com, where he actually hired Second City Works on a couple of occasions. Second City Works now does more than four hundred engagements a year, half with Fortune 1000 companies. Tom and his team are focused on refining The Second City's unique capabilities—creating funny short-form content and using improv to develop vital skills in businesspeople—to help companies communicate, collaborate, and innovate better in a web-first, social-everything world.